Remains of loggia at Dunluce Castle, Co Antrim

THE CASTLES

OF ULSTER

Mike Salter

FOLLY PUBLICATIONS

ACKNOWLEDGEMENTS

The illustrations in this book are mostly the product of the author's own site surveys since 1971. Plans redrawn from his field note books are mostly reproduced to scales of 1:400 for keeps, tower houses, stronghouses and the like, and 1:800 for courtyard castles and bawns, whilst earthworks and large bawns are shown at 1:2000. The author would like to acknowledge with thanks the assistance of the following individuals. Max Barfield drove on the 1992 trip and took the photos of Inch, the gatehouse and keep at Dundrum, the loggia at Dunluce, and the photo of Greencastle, Co Down on the front cover. Helen Thomas drove the author around all nine counties of Ulster except Co Down in 2003 and checked the text. Ken McLeod provided accommodation, transport for fieldwork in Down and Armagh, much help and support, and also the photograph of Buncrana (along with other pictures not used). Thanks are also due to the staffs of the Northern Ireland National Monument Record in Belfast and to the archaeological record section of the Department of the Environment and Local Government in Dublin, who both privided much information.

AUTHOR'S NOTES

This book is one of a series of five volumes superseding the author's previous work Castles and Stronghouses of Ireland published in 1993 and now out of print. It is part of a series of books about castles in the British Isles all in a similar style with plans on a set of metric common scales allowing useful comparisons of sizes, wall thicknesses, etc. It is recommended that visitors use the Ordnance Survey 1:50,000 maps to locate the monuments, and grid references are given in the gazetteers. The book is indeed intended as a portable field guide giving as much information and illustrative material as possible, especially for buildings about which little has previously appeared in print. The aim has been to mention (where known) owners or custodians of buildings who erected or altered parts of them and those involved in dramatic events such as rebellions or sieges. Owners and occupants whose lives had little effect on the condition of the buildings are generally not mentioned nor, are most 19th and 20th century events or myths or legends.

Each of the main levels of a building is called a storey in this book, the basement or ground level room (usually a storage cellar) being the first storey. Sleeping lofts squeezed under vaults are usually treated as separate storeys if they have their own direct access from the main staircase. Attics mainly or entirely within roof spaces are generally mentioned separately, buildings described as being of so many storeys plus an attic.

All dimensions are given in metres, and were taken at or near ground level, but above the plinth if there is one. The majority of the quoted measurements were taken personally on site by the author. On plans the original work is shown black, post-1800 work is stippled and alterations and additions of intermediate periods are shown hatched.

ABOUT THE AUTHOR

Mike Salter is 50 and has been a professional writer and publisher since 1988. He is particularly interested in the planning and layout of medieval buildings and has a huge collection of plans of castles and churches he has measured during tours throughout all parts of the British Isles since 1968. He has particularly specialised in the study of tower houses and fortified houses in England, Wales, Scotland and Ireland, hence his determination to produce this new series of five books about Irish castles. Wolverhampton born and bred, Mike now lives in an old cottage beside the Malvern Hills. His other interests include walking, maps, railways, board games, morris dancing, playing percussion instruments and calling dances with an occasional folk group.

Gatehouse at Dundrum, Co Down

CONTENTS

A map of surviving castles appears inside of the front cover

INTRODUCTION

Forts built of limestone blocks laid without mortar or having stockades upon earth ramparts were common in Ireland during the Dark Ages but castles as the Normans knew them were introduced by them when they invaded Ireland in the late 1160s. The earliest castles built in the province of Ulster seem to have been those erected by John de Courcy during his rapid take over of Antrim and Down in 1177. Initially the castles built by de Courcy and his followers were mostly structures of earth and wood since buildings of mortared stone require months or years of relative peace and prosperity to construct. Commonly earth was dug from a circular ditch and piled within it to form a mound called a motte which bore a wooden house or tower forming the lord's residence within a small palisaded enclosure. Often there was a base court or bailey around the motte or on one side of it. This enclosure was normally defended by a rampart bearing a stockade and a surrounding ditch, and would contain a hall, chapel, kitchen, and the usual range or barns and workshops required by any farming establishment, all built of wood. Castles of this type vary in size and shape and often used natural spurs or promontories. Over a hundred are known to have existed in Ulster, most of them being in Antrim and Down.

In the 1180s de Courcy began building a stronger and more permanent castle of stone on a rocky headland at Carrickfergus and in the 1190s he is thought to have begun another at Dundrum. Both have modestly sized courts surrounded by fairly thin curtain walls although Carrickfergus also has a square tower keep, a building containing a hall over cellars reached only from above and a private room over the hall, the rooms being lighted by small round-headed windows. In 1204 Henry de Lacy took over the de Courcy possessions and was created Earl of Ulster, but in 1210 King John took over both castles. Both castles were returned to the de Lacys in 1227 and Dundrum was then given a gatehouse and a circular tower keep, a type less practical for habitation but stronger since it had no blind or vulnerable corners, whilst Carrickfergus was given an outer ward with a twin round-towered gatehouse. Around this time a hall keep was built at Greencastle in Down, a type with sufficient length for a private room and public hall end-to-end on the same level (above cellars) instead of one above the other. This castle was strengthened in the 1260s by a surrounding court with U-shaped corner towers. There are only scanty remains of several small 13th century castles at Clough, Court McMartin, Doonbought and Doonmore, all in Antrim. Thought to have been cavalry depots, they had thin stone walls surrounding small courts which presumably contained lean-to wooden buildings. Also in Antrim is Castle Carra, a tiny hall house containing just one living room over a dark cellar. Other remains (both in Down) are a tiny tower and excavated evidence of a vanished hall on a motte at Clough and a ruinous hall keep with traces of an adjoining polygonal court at Seefin. The word keep, incidentally, is more recent and medieval charters and chronicles refer such a building as a great tower (magnum turris).

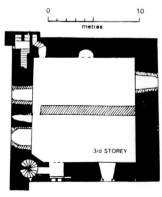

Carrickfergus: plan of keep

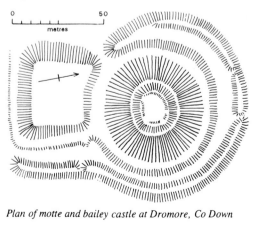

Plan of motte and bailey castle at Dromore, Co Down

Motte and later folly at Donaghadee, Co Down

Castles known to date from the 14th century are rare in Ireland and Ulster contains only three of note. The de Burgh family, who had succeeded the de Lacys as earls of Ulster, erected at Greencastle in Donegal a substantial court extending between a polygonal main tower and a gatehouse with two polygonal towers. After the murder of the heirless Earl William in 1333 as part of a family feud, Anglo-Norman influence in Ulster rapidly declined except for in a few places along the Antrim and Down coast. From the early 13th century until 1607 the most powerful families in the rest of Ulster were the O'Donnells ruling Tir Chonaill and the O'Neills of Tir Eoghain. In the 1360s Henry O'Neill built Harry Avery's Castle, a building with a polygonal court which could only be reached (on foot) by narrow stairs within a three storey tower looking like (but not functioning as) a gatehouse, since it had two round towers facing the field. Just a fragment remains of what may be a second castle of this type and date at Elagh to the west of Londonderry. More impressive are the two circular towers at Dunluce which formed the corners of a court probably built in the 14th or early 15th century by the MacDonnells.

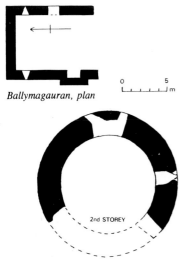

Ballymagauran, plan

Plan of Cloughoughter Castle

Corner tower at Greencastle, Co Down

Greencastle, Co Donegal

The tower at Harry Averys was an early tower house, probably the first in Ulster of a type that became numerous in the 15th and 16th centuries, although tower houses were never as dense on the ground in Ulster as they were in other parts of Ireland and very few of the tower houses built by the Gaelic-speaking native Irish chiefs in Ulster remain anything like complete. Unlike the earlier keeps and hall houses the tower houses normally had entrances at ground level and nearly all of them had at least one main level covered by a stone vault. The space immediately under the vault was usually used as a dark loft either for storage or for sleeping space for those of lesser rank. Towers in the English-speaking coastal areas are generally modest in size and wall-thickness and consequently many of them needed projecting turrets to accommodate spiral staircases and latrines. Several examples have these projecting turrets on the same side so that it was possible to link them at the top by a flying arch behind which was a machicolation protecting the entrance at the foot of the staircase. The plain rectangular towers without projections in the Gaelic areas tend to have thicker walls and be of greater size, those at Donegal and Enniskellen being very substantial buildings. Some of these towers have one end wall thickened to contain a tier of vaulted rooms over the entrance. Above a vault the main bodies of these towers have thinner walls giving larger rooms and consequently they had a different layout, often with a hall at the top of the tower and the lord's apartment halfway up, whilst towers in the English-speaking areas conform to the layout normal in tower houses in England and Scotland with private rooms at the top and a more public hall halfway up. Another important difference was the presence of square bartizans on tall inverted pyramidal corbels with machicolations between them on the top corners of the Gaelic towers. Both in the English and Gaelic areas the towers usually had pointed-arched doorways, upper windows with ogival-arched lights either singly or in pairs, and internal machicolations known as murder holes covering the entrance lobbies are common.

There is very little documentary evidence to help with dating medieval tower houses in Ulster since many of the records were destroyed during the wars of the 17th century, whilst some plan-forms and architectural features remained in fashion for two centuries. Circumstantial evidence and analogy with other Irish buildings suggest many of the towers in the English speaking parts are early to mid 15th century, whilst the towers in the Gaelic areas are late 15th to early 16th century. Large mullioned windows, especially with hoodmoulds, the presence of small gunloops, and the lack of a vault over any of the main rooms are signs of a late 16th or early 17th century date. Towers in Gaelic areas seem to have lacked fireplaces, the topmost halls being heated by central braziers with the smoke escaping through a louvre in the roof, so the presence of fireplaces suggests either a late date or evidence of a later remodelling.

Many of the towers had small accompanying courts known as bawns, sometimes with walls thick enough to carry wall-walks as at Doe, the only place in the Gaelic parts of Ulster where a pre-17th century bawn survives in anything like its original state, complete with flankers and corner bartizans, plus an usual casemate flanking a small inner enclosure by the tower. A more fragmentary bawn with two round flankers remains with along with a very late (early to mid 17th century) tower house at Termon. Around the coast there are very fragmentary remains of a number of castles where a main tower facing to landward contained the entrance to a bawn behind.

In medieval castles walls were often whitewashed both inside and out, the whitewashing making the best of the limited light admitted through narrow window loops. Glass was uncommon in medieval castles and windows had shutters opened inwards whenever the weather allowed it. Both public and private rooms might have latrines within the walls and wall paintings of biblical, allegorical or historic scenes, or heraldry, and similar motifs would appear on tapestries and other wall hangings, whilst occasionally a room might have the luxury of wainscoting.

The sort of privacy we now take for granted simply did not exist in medieval castles. Even those of high rank often had attendants sleeping in the same room or in the passage giving access to it, although the lordly bed was usually screened off or curtained. Many of the occupants of a castle slept in the main hall, which was usually the warmest room. Irish tower houses rarely have separate kitchens so either cooking was done in a separate outbuilding (although there is little surviving evidence of this) or upon the fires in the main rooms. In the 16th century both English and Spanish nobles found Irish cooking to be well below the standards they were use to. Floors were covered with rushes and those not in the form of planks set upon beams were of clay or rammed earth rather than flagstones. Furniture was sparse and of the simplest kind. Only the lord and his family might have individual chairs in their room or in the hall, but the latter room would contain tables and benches and there would be several chests used both for seating and for the storing of clothes, plate, utensils and valuables.

Portmuck Castle, Co Antrim

Seafin Castle, Co Down   *Red Bay Castle, Co Antrim*

Shane's Castle, Co Antrim

In the mid 16th century the O'Donnells of Tir Chonaill and the O'Neills of Tir Eoghain were persuaded to make at least a nominal submittance to the English Crown and their lands recognised as earldoms. The 1570s saw English attempts to oust the MacDonnells and Clannaboy O'Neills of Antrim. The English seizure of the Maguire lands in Fermanagh in the 1590s started a war during which the O'Neills and O'Donnells brought much of Ireland under their authority until Lord Mountjoy arrived in 1600 with a vast army. The earls submitted in 1603 and their lands were shired into counties Armagh, Derry, Donegal, and Tyrone. Since the earls' position became untenable they fled to Spain in 1607, leaving King James I free to grant much of Ulster to London guilds and loyal Protestant families, particularly Presbyterian lowland Scots. The new lords or their agents (for many of the new landowners were absentees) were obliged to erect new houses with adjoining bawns or courts to protect their plantations. Some of the houses are of three storeys but many were thinly walled and only had two storeys (living rooms below and bedrooms above) with servants rooms in attics in the roofs. Intended to offer resistance only to short-lived raids by malefactors rather than full-scale sieges, the bawns mostly have flanking bastions (known as flankers) containing gunloops. The flankers can be circular, as at Portora, which had a full set or four, or Brackfield, where there are two at diagonally opposite corners, but often the flankers were square so that those adjoining the house could contain useful upper rooms with fireplaces. Fort Stewart has a spearhead-shaped flanker, a smaller version of some of the bastions of the contemporary fortified towns. The bawn walls themselves often have gunloops at ground level, all of them being too thin to support wall-walks. The older castles in the Gaelic areas of Ulster were wrecked during the late 16th century wars and many were subsequently dismantled for their materials so that very few of them survive. Those at Donegal and Enniskillen were taken over by incoming families and remodelled with new upper parts with large windows. The surveyor Francis Pynnar, who travelled around Ulster in 1619, gives us an idea of the extent of the plantation by telling us that it involved the construction of nearly 2000 houses, 107 castles with bawns, 19 castles without bawns, and 43 bawns containing only modest houses. Several towns were also provided with walls and bastions although very little survives of them apart from the almost complete circuit at Derry and fragments at Carrickfergus.

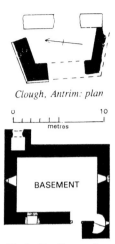

Clough, Antrim: plan

0 |⌞⌞⌞⌞⌞⌞| 10
    metres

BASEMENT

Ringhaddy, Down: plan

Castle Skreen, Co Down

Dromore, Co Down

Some of the plantation bawns and fortified houses managed to withstand attacks by the Confederate Irish during the rebellion of 1641 but many were captured and burnt either then or in the years that followed. Others suffered during the fighting of 1689-91. By the 18th century most of those not already in ruins were abandoned in favour of more comfortable residences elsewhere. Others were remodelled or incorporated in newer mansions, although some of these are now in turn long abandoned. Still in use as residences or public buildings are Ballygally, Galgorm, Glenarm, and Redhall in Antrim, Killyleagh and Kirkistown in Down, and Augher in Tyrone. Also roofed, but now as unoccupied ancient monuments are Audleys, Ardglass (Jordans), Carrickfergus (gatehouse and keep only) Castle Ward, Doe & Donegal (tower houses and bawn flankers only), Enniskillen, Kilclief, and Strangford. Over a hundred other places have substantial ruins, whilst other places now only have slight remains or are now sites without any remains.

Killyleagh Castle, Co Down

Castle Balfour, Co Fermanagh

FURTHER READING

Archaeological Survey of County Down, 1966
Archaeological Survey of Donegal, Brian Lacy, 1983.
Buildings of County Antrim, C.E.B.Brett, 1996.
Castles In Ireland, Tom NcNeill, 1997.
Historic Monuments of Northern Ireland, H.M.S.O, 1983.
The Medieval Castles of Ireland, David Sweetman, 1999.
Shell Guide to Ireland, Lord Killanin & M. Duignan, 1969
Buildings of North West Ulster, Alistair Rowan, 1979.
Guide pamphlets exist for Ardglass (Jordan's), Audleys,
  Carrickfergus, Donegal, Dundrum, Dungiven, Dunluce,
  Enniskellen, Greencastle (Co Down), Monea.
See also the annual Proceedings of the Royal Irish Academy,
  the Journal of the Royal Society of Antiquaries of Ireland,
  Ulster Journal of Archaeology, and Medieval Archaeology.

Movanagher,
Co Londonderry:
old sketch

ACCESS TO THE CASTLES

The following codes appear after the O.S. grid references in the gazetteers. They give only an indication since access arrangements may change from time to time, as may the amount of vegetation obscuring distant views, whilst some monuments may be closed during the winter months. Sites not given a code lie on private land and can only be seen by obtaining prior permission from the landowners. Only very occasionally will a courteous request for access by those with a genuine interest in ancient buildings be refused outright, although some owners may forbid visitors to enter ruins considered to be dangerous. Visitors should in all cases close any gates that they need to open, ensure that their dogs do not cause any kind of nuisance to the farmers or their animals, and generally follow the rule of taking away nothing but photographs and leaving nothing but footprints.

A -   Free access on foot to the whole site at any time. Mostly sites in State care.
B -   Free access on foot at any time to the exterior only. Mostly sites in State care.
C -   Private, but clearly visible from public road, path, or other open space.
D -   Private, but distant view usually possible from road, path, or other open space.
E -   Open to the public (fee usually payable) during certain hours.
G -   Private, but a well-used courtesy access is currently normally possible.
H -   Buildings in use as hotels, shops, museums, etc. Exterior access usually possible.

Dunluce Castle, Co Antrim

0   10
⌊ ⌊ ⌊ ⌊ ⌊ ⌋ m

Walshestown: plan

0   5
⌊ ⌊ ⌊ ⌊ ⌊ ⌋ m

Kirkistown: plan

BALLYGALLEY   D372078   C

James Shaw of Greenock built this L-plan tower in 1625. Scottish in design, it contains a hall over two vaulted cellars, then two bedrooms side-by-side, and attic rooms in the roof. There are conical-roofed bartizans both on the main block and on the wing which contains an extra bedroom reached by a narrow stair corbelled out over the re-entrant angle. Below this the wing contains the main spiral stair connecting the three main levels with the entrance at its foot. Most of the windows have been either renewed or widened.

BELFAST   J339743

Belfast is first mentioned in the late 15th century, when it had a Clannaboy O'Neill castle commanding the river crossing at the mouth of the Lagan. The castle was granted to Sir Arthur Chichester in 1603 and the town around it was incorporated as a Parliamentary borough in 1613. Arthur's brother Edward was the ancestor of the Marquess of Donegal and Lord O'Neill who assumed the Clannaboy name in 1855. Nothing survives either of the castle or of the town walls built in response to the rebellion of 1641, although defences had been mooted earlier. The area enclosed by the walls measured 600m by 500m and required nine or ten angled flanking bastions.

Carrickfergus Castle

Carrickfergus: hall window

Town gateway at Carrickfergus

Ballygalley Castle

Carrickfergus Castle

CARRICKFERGUS   J414872   E

In the 1180s John de Courcy, an adventurer from Somerset who conquered most of eastern Ulster, began the construction of a polygonal curtain wall around a court 44m by 26m on the end of a low rocky promontory. Shortly afterwards work began on four storey tower keep 16.5m square and 27m high within the northern end of the court. The twin cellars (with 15th century vaults) were originally only reached from the hall above. One cellar retains an original loop and contains the well. Above the hall was a more private hall and then on top the lord's bedroom. The south corners have projections to help contain respectively the staircase adjacent to the original entrance on the east side and a tier of latrines. Both projections die into the wallface below the summit, where these corners rise as low turrets. In 1204 de Courcy was defeated at Carrickfergus by Hugh de Lacy, who became Earl of Ulster. He completed the keep and a hall on the east side of the court, now only represented by two narrow round-headed windows in the outer wall. In 1210 King John took over the castle and added the middle ward strengthening the north and east sides. The much remodelled east wall remains together with a boldly projecting tower 5m by 4.5m containing round-arched embrasures with triple arrow-loops, but the northern wall with its polygonal flanking tower and gateway was later destroyed down to footings only revealed again during excavations and conservation work in the 1950s.

Earl Hugh de Lacy later recovered the castle and between 1226 and 1242 he is thought to have had the remainder of the rock enclosed to form an outer ward 40m wide with one small square flanking turret on the west side. The north end was closed off by a gatehouse with two circular towers about 12m in diameter flanking the passageway. A second portcullis, a new vault and external in internal machicolations were provided just before or some time after the long siege by Edward Bruce in 1315-16. In front was a pit crossed by a removable bridge. An upper room in the east tower has a two-light east window of c1200 reset probably elsewhere in the castle. Although it contained a mint established in 1251, the castle was often inadequately garrisoned and maintained in the later medieval period, and it was captured and damaged in 1384 by Niall Mor O'Neill. By then it had passed permanently into the hands of the Crown and it was retained as a state fortress, prison and administrative centre until 1928 when it was transferred to the Ministry of Finance for preservation as an ancient monument.

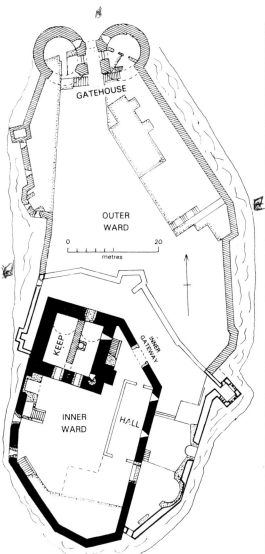

Plan of Carrickfergus Castle

Chapel window at Carrickfergus

Keep at Carrickfergus

The castle was remodelled for defence by artillery in the mid 16th century, when wide-mouthed ports partly of brick were inserted in the outer walls and the lower rooms of the gatehouse towers were then filled up with earth to provide a solid floor for mounting cannon. The inner parts of the towers were then pulled down to provide easier access and the outer wall-heads lowered and made suitable for an upper battery. In 1575 Somhairle Buidhe MacDonnell overthrew the castle garrison in revenge for the burning of 600 defenceless Scots by the Earl of Essex, and in 1597 the MacDonnells ambushed and beheaded the castle governor. In 1602, Con, chief of the Clannoboy O'Neills, escaped from the castle by means of a rope smuggled in by his wife within a huge cheese.

William III landed beside Carrickfergus Castle in June 1690 after the Duke of Schomberg had captured it from James II's forces. It was then left to decay until in January 1754 a 15m length of the curtain wall fell down at the southern end. This breach was still open in 1760 when Commodore Thurot landed 800 French troops from three ships and assaulted the castle. The garrison of five officers and 230 men, mostly raw recruits, repelled three assaults even though they ran out of bullets and had to fire their tunic buttons and then use bayonets, bricks and stones. Eventually, with no hope of relief, they surrendered and marched out with the honours of war, having delayed Thurot's return home long enough for him to be intercepted, defeated and killed by the Royal Navy off the Isle of Man. The breach was subsequently filled with a huge solid gun platform and several others were created on the east side. Anti-submarine guns were mounted on these platforms in the 1914-18 war and the keep basement was used as an air-raid shelter during the 1939-45 war.

Carrickfergus was the chief port of Ulster in the medieval period and many of the wealthier merchants built themselves tower houses like those of Ardglass and Carlingford. Nothing survives of any of them but a late 16th century sketch shows a dozen of them, including two almost adjoining one another and one which was circular. There also remain from c1610-25 a gateway with a moulded arch, sections of a thin wall originally backed by an earth rampart, and the northernmost of four angled bastions (there were also two demi-bastions where the walls ran out to the shore).

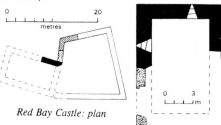

Red Bay Castle: plan

Plan of Castle Dobbs

Castle Carra

Castle Chichester

CASTLE CARRA   D248335   D

This small early hall house measuring 8.5m by 6m over walls 1.4m thick containing just one upper room over a dark basement with a battered base is said to have been the scene of the murder of Sean "The Proud" O'Neill by the MacDonnells in 1567. The upper level has two windows in wide embrasures, an entrance facing east and remains of a stair leading up in the north wall.

CASTLE CHICHESTER   J476920   C

In the grounds of one of a row of houses near the shore is a three storey tower built c1604 by Sir Moses Hill. Roughly a cube of 8.4m, it has a machicolation over the doorway, which, like all the lower windows, has been blocked up in recent times.

CASTLE UPTON   J228859

Sir Humphrey Norton's house of Temple Patrick dated 1611 on a doorcase was renamed Castle Upton after being sold to Captain Henry Upton in 1625. The Uptons later became Viscounts Templetown. The square three storey main block has round turrets at the NE and SW corners. The house was given a hipped roof and extended northwards in 1788 by Robert Adam and the SW turret was later given an embattled fourth storey.

CLOUGH   D095147   C

The de Mandevilles' motte and bailey castle on a basalt rock outcrop was later refortified in stone by the MacQuillans. It passed to the MacDonnells and was rebuilt in the early 17th century as a Plantation stronghouse. The castle was captured by the Confederate Catholics in 1641 and destroyed during the Cromwellian campaign of 1650. The only remains are two fragments of a forework of some kind added to the west of footings of a fragment of a 1.6m thick curtain wall probably of 13th century date.

Castle Upton

Castle Chichester

2nd STOREY

1st STOREY

Castle Carra

Clough Castle

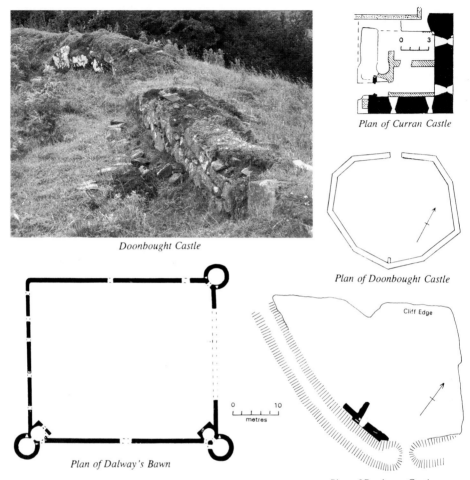

Plan of Curran Castle

Doonbought Castle

Plan of Doonbought Castle

Plan of Dalway's Bawn

Plan of Dunineny Castle

CURRAN   D413016   A

There were originally three towers guarding Larne harbour. Two of them were called Curran and Olderflete and there is confusion as to which one has survived. The third tower was called Tchevet. The lowest level of the three storey tower 10.6m square over walls 2m thick was later subdivided with barrel vaults and an oven some of the original double-splayed loops being blocked in the process. The entrance gave onto the foot of a straight stair in the west wall, which along with the north wall is destroyed to the footings.

DALWAY'S BAWN   J443915   C

Named after John Dalloway, who built it in 1609, this bawn with a wall 0.9m thick and 5m high enclosing a rectangle 40m by 33m is fairly well preserved, despite the modern windows pierced through to light the later farmbuildings inside. Three corners have flankers 5.5m in diameter, two of which, adjoining a road, have conical roofs and three storeys of rooms with renewed mullioned windows connected by wooden stairs in turrets placed diagonally on the inner corners. There is a ring over the entrance gateway.

Curran Castle

Dalway's Bawn

DOONBOUGHT   D108131

The lower parts of a 13th century 1.1m thick wall surround a polygonal court measuring 26m by 22m thought to have contained wooden buildings. A ditch lies 10m beyond the entrance on the north. There are drystone outer defences on the south side.

DOONMORE   D173428   C

Excavations on a commanding rocky outcrop with footings of a wall around a court 18m by 12m found traces of timber revetments and postholes of a timber tower 3.6m square along with a 12th or 13th century cooking-pot. There are indications of small outworks at a slightly lower level to the north and east. A crannog lies in the lough further east.

DUNINENY   D113419   A

Dun an Aonaigh (Fort of the Public Assembly) lies on a 60m high promontory isolated by a ditch behind a caravan site just NW of Ballycastle. One of the earliest MacDonnell castles, this was the main seat of Somhairle Buidhe MacDonnell from his accession in 1558 until his death in 1589. Facing the ditch is the lower part of a building with a front wall 8m long pierced by a gateway near its west end. Stubs of curtain walls adjoin each end but there are no obvious traces of any other buildings.

Doonmore Castle

Dunineny Castle

DUNLUCE   C905414   E

This castle has a very strong site on a rock pierced by a natural cave at sea-level in which galleys could be concealed. Two circular towers 9m in diameter on the east side and the 1.8m thick landward-facing south wall are relics of a castle built thought to date from the late 14th or early 15th century, although the castle is not mentioned in any records prior to the early 16th century, when it was the seat of the MacQuillans. The towers have doorways at ground level and stairs curving round within the walls to reach the upper rooms. The NE tower overlies a souterrain or rock-cut hiding place of the Early Christian period, proof of early usage of the site.

The castle passed to Somhairle Buidhe MacDonnell, who surrendered it to Sean "The Proud" O'Neill in 1565 but recovered it after Sean was murdered in 1567. Lord Deputy Sir John Perrot inflicted serious damage to the castle with "a culverin and two sakers of brass" during a siege in 1584. Afterwards the landward-facing wall was mostly rebuilt and provided with two large gun-ports with an open loggia behind, whilst a new gatehouse with a passageway flanked by long guard room and conical-roofed bartizans on the outer corners was built at the SW corner. Cannon are thought to have been obtained from the Girona, an Armada galleass wrecked nearby in 1588. See photos on pages 1 and 10.

Somhairle's son Sir Randal remained loyal to the English Crown and James I rewarded him with large estate and titles, including the earldom of Antrim created in 1620. At Dunluce Sir Randal probably built the large unfortified outer court providing extra accommodation, offices and outbuildings on the mainland. He certainly filled most of the main courtyard with a huge new hall 28m long by 10m wide with three bay windows on the west side. A buttery adjoins to the north with a kitchen wing with fireplaces and ovens east of it, and there is a balancing SE wing at the other end of the hall which contained a wide timber staircase to the bedrooms above. Further north a lower yard was created with long ranges of offices, workshops, and lodgings on the west, east and north sides. It was probably the north wall of the latter that collapsed into the sea in 1639, killing several servants. The castle was besieged by the rebel Irish in 1641 and in 1642 the Scottish Covenanter General Munro arrested the 2nd Earl of Antrim whilst being entertained at the castle. It was subsequently little used. A new house further inland was begun at the insistence of the 2nd Earl's wife, who disliked the noise of the sea. The house may never have been occupied and very little of it now remains. The 7th Earl transferred the ruins to the state in 1928 for preservation as an ancient monument.

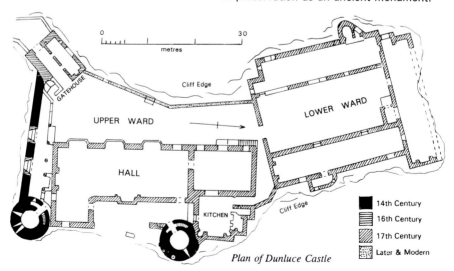

14th Century
16th Century
17th Century
Later & Modern

Plan of Dunluce Castle

Dunluce Castle

DUNSEVERICK   C988446   A

One side of a coastal headland thought to have been a royal seat during the Dark Ages is a small promontory 13m long with footings of a thin breastwork. On the promontory neck is a fragmentary 16th century tower measuring 6.7m by 6m over walls 1.3m thick. It was held by the O'Kanes under the MacQuillans and was captured in 1565 by Sean "The Proud" O'Neill. After Giolla O'Kane was executed by the Cromwellians in 1653 the castle was dismantled and abandoned.

GALGORM   D081023   C

A remodelling of 1832 for the Earl of Mountcashell has resulted in curved gables being added to the house of four storeys and attics built in the 1630s by Dr Alexander Colville within a bawn established in 1618-19 by Sir Faithful Fortescue. Neither the parts of the bawn incorporated in outbuildings nor the house retain any defensive features.

KILWAUGHTER   D356015

The west wing of the impressive castellated ruined house of 1807 is a very ruined early 17th century T-plan tower house of four storeys. The wing contained the entrance and staircase but the features are obscured by debris, alterations and partial collapse.

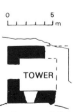

Dunseverick

Dunseverick Castle

Kinbane Castle

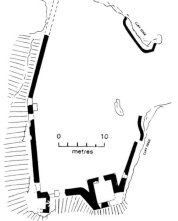

Plan of Kinbane Castle

KINBANE   D088448   A

In 1558 Colla Dubh MacDonnell, elder brother of Somhairle Buidhe, died in his castle of Kinbane begun in 1547. A tower 6.5m square with just a single room over a basement and gables to east and west but open battlements on the other sides lies on the south side of an irregular shaped bawn 40m long by 24m wide set on the neck of a headland. Much of the bawn west wall remains, together with part of a square SW corner turret, between which and the main tower was the bawn gateway. On the east side the bawn only needed a low breastwork above the sheer drop to the sea.

LISBURN   J269643   A

In Castle Gardens, off Castle Street, is a gateway dated 1677, the only relic of a castle built in 1627 by Sir Fulke Conway, who was granted Lisburn (then called Lisnagarvey) in 1609. The town and castle were damaged by the rebel Irish in 1641 and were destroyed by an accidental fire in 1707.

RED BAY   D243262   D

A motte erected by the Bissetts above the coast road bears a fragment of the south wall of a tower of three low storeys about 12.6m long by 7.8m wide. The moulded corbelled courses at the summit and the roll-moulded jambs of windows show a Scottish influence. Adjoining it is a corner of a crudely built bawn 12m across. The bailey to the south has fragments of a thin wall on the west side and a sheer cliff to the east and south. The site was fortified by Sir James MacDonnell in 1561 but was ravaged by Sean O'Neill in 1565 and the ruins may represent what was begun in 1568 by Somhairle Buidhe MacDonnell. His elder son James dismantled the castle in 1597 but the younger son Randal restored it in 1604. It was destroyed by the Cromwellian garrison of Carrickfergus in 1652. See p14

REDHALL   J451951

This looks like an 18th century house of three storeys over a basement only exposed on one side, but fine ceilings inside go back to when Sir William Edmonstone built a new house here c1610 to replace a Clannaboy O'Neill castle. The insurgents of 1798 broke in, hoping to obtain Richard Gervase's gun collection, but he had removed all the firing pins.

SHANE'S   J116880

The east end of the mansion burnt in 1815 is an O'Neill tower measuring 8.6m by 7.3m over walls 1m thick. The adjoining round tower is later, as are remains of extensive outbuildings and platform by Lough Neagh. See p8.

Portmuck: plan

OTHER CASTLE REMAINS IN COUNTY ANTRIM

ANTRIM J145867 Demesne contains motte and bailey noted in Pipe Rolls for 1211-12. Nearby house of 1602 rebuilt in 1816, burnt in 1922, demolished except a turret.
BALLYLOUGH C947374 West wall with doorway and north wall of McQuillan tower.
BROOKHILL J204662 Slight remains behind present house of bawn built in 1611 by Sir Faulke Conway, captured by the O'Neills in 1641.
BRUCE'S CASTLE D163515 Slight traces of walls of bawn and tower backing onto cliff edge above coast of Rathlin Island.
CARNCASTLE D381080 Low wall 1m thick surrounds three sides of space 9m by 7.5m, either a tower basement or small open court, set on a low offshore rock.
CASTLE DOBBS J443907 East wall 9.8m long and 1.3m thick stands three storeys high of tower of 1600 near later mansion. See page 14.
CASTLE ROBIN J248686 Fragments three storeys high of house 12m by 6.3m built on site of bailey 26m by 13m of adjoining motte rising up to 7m to a summit 9m across.
CLOGHANMURRY D083374 Low fragment of wall on edge of summit of high motte.
CONNOR J152969 Traces of battered curtain wall base at SW corner of pentagonal ditched platform 39m across. Possible seat of O'Flynn kings of Ui Tuirtre in 1260s.
COURT McMARTIN D235276 Modern house within strongly sited platform with very overgrown traces of thin curtain wall (best preserved on SW).
DEERPARK J142841 Motte and bailey with stone revetted ditches built in 1190s by Roger de Courcy.
GLENARM D309151 House dated 1756 on site of house begun by Randal MacDonnell, Earl of Antrim, in 1603 and burnt by General Munro's Covenanters in 1642. 1636 datestone reset on 19th century outer gateway. 1720 service wing survives.
KILROOT J450895 Much altered and thinly walled house and bawn built c1602-6 by Bishop Humpston of Down. Dovecote built over north flanker. No defensive features.
LAYD D246289 Tower 7.8m by 7.2m at west end of church. Very ruinous domestic upper storeys for priest over vaulted basement with doorways at each end.
PORTMUCK D461024 Lowest level of tower 6m square with vaulted 2m wide central passage and latrine chute at one corner beside farm. See page 7.
TOOME H989902 Tower east wall and part of bastion found by excavation in 1991.
CASTLE SITES: Ballintoy D039448, Ballycarry D153512, Ballyginniff J111809, Ballymagarry C894402, Ballymoney C946253, Ballyvaston J302813, Broughshane D151066, Castle Culbert D135390, Castle Lug J374844, Crebilly D143027, Cushlancarragh D244277, Duncarbit D143354, Kilraghts D015257, Knockcairn J201743, Layd D244277, Lisanoure D066243, Malone J321691 & 335713, Portglone C977037, Portmore J121684, Portrush C858406, Rathmore J182873, Retreat D204242, Staffordstown J037867, Whitehouse J351808
OTHER MOTTES (with baileys *): Ballycastle 121409, Ballyclover J227906, Ballycarry J454946, Ballydown D437006, Ballyhackett D351072, Ballymather J249799, Ballymena D169092, Ballyrobin J184827, Capecastle D084374, Carn Graney J270839, Doonan D274141, Droagh D381062, Drumard 960278, Drumlane 118056, Drumnadonaghy D358017, Dunamoy J263944, Glenarm D300120, Magherahoney* D077298, Marronstown J386899, Milebush J416886, Milltown D356095, Nettlebush J204878, Skeagh 314059 Randalstown* J096875, Rathenraw* J171874, Shaneoguestown J190843.

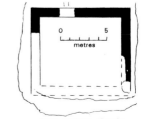

Plan of Carn Castle

GAZETTEER OF CASTLES IN COUNTY ARMAGH

CASTLE RAW   H927529   C

Most of the lower parts of the walls remain of a cruciform house built in 1618, and there is a higher fragment of the north wall of the 7.7m wide west wing with windows for two upper storeys over a low basement partly below ground level.

CHARLEMONT   H854558

Commanding a crossing of the Blackwater on the boundary with Tyrone are traces of the earthworks of a square fort with four arrowhead shaped bastions erected during Lord Mountjoy's campaign of 1602 against Hugh O'Neill. It was finally completed in 1624, although outworks were added in 1673 and the surviving gateway bearing the Caulfield arms is probably late 18th century. The fort was captured by Sir Phelim O'Neill in 1641, and, strengthened with new outworks in 1642, it withstood an attack by the Scottish army led by General Leslie. It remained in O'Neill hands until captured by the Cromwellian commander Venables in 1650. It was stormed by a Williamite force commanded by the Duke of Shomberg in 1690 and remained a British garrison post until 1858. The fine three storey house with numerous bay windows within the fort was the home of the Caulfields, later made Lords Charlemont, but it and a later barrack block were demolished in 1922 after being burnt by guerillas.

MOYRY   J058147   E

The road between Dundalk and Newry is commanded by a three storey tower 7.3m square over walls 1.2m thick erected by Lord Mountjoy in 1601. Evidence of the hurried construction is the lack of vaults or cut stone, the corners being rounded and pierced by four of the seven loops in the lowest level, which also has an entrance doorway facing north. The upper storeys have fireplaces and latrine recesses in the west wall and windows on the other sides. The tower lay within a bawn about 28m long by 17m wide now deliniated by a low cliff on the south, a 2m high and 6m long fragment of walling on the east and a 17m length of the base of the north wall incorporated into a field boundary.

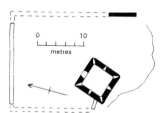

Plan of Moyry Castle

Castle Raw

Moyry Castle

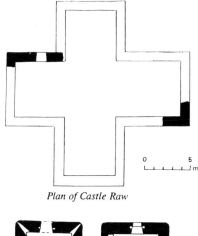

Plan of Castle Raw

Plans of Moyry Castle

Gatehouse at Charlemont

OTHER CASTLE REMAINS IN COUNTY ARMAGH

DERRYWARRAGH H929643 Chimney breast with ornamental stacks alone remains of stronghouse. A proposal to build a large new fort here in the 1680s came to nothing.
GOSFORD H954393 Traces of bawn 36m by 24 with four flankers. House had timber upper storey.
MAGHERNAHELY J040286 Remains of bawn in convent garden.
The fort at Clare Castle is of late date. The house of the 1650s at Richhill is planned for flanking fire but has no gunloops or other defensive features.

CASTLE SITES IN COUNTY ARMAGH

ARDGONNELL H739375 Part of O'Neill tower remodelled in late 17th century probably by Sir Robert Hamilton stood until 1950s. Had one round bartizan. Site now built over.
BRANNOOCK J058410 Site of Sir Toby Poinz' 24m square bawn.
DRUMBANAGHER J054364 Site of Garret Moore's bawn measuring 33m by 27m with two flankers.
GRASDRUMMAN H966147 Site of 15th century O'Neill tower and later bawn burnt in 1642, but rebuilt later. Cleared away c1710 by Patrick Murray.
HAMILTON'S H950443 Site of John Hamilton's bawn with three ranges inside. Burnt in 1641, sold in 1704 and later replaced by a barracks.
KILLEEN H903427 Site of Claud Hamilton's 24m square bawn with circular corner flankers.
MAGHON J003518 House of 1846-7 to north of site of castle of Workman family.
ROWANTREES H968494 Site of bawn built in 1641.
TANDRAGEE J030462 No remains survive of the tower house of the O'Hanlons.
Other castle sites: Armagh H875452, Creevekeeran H785371, Drumilly H911513, Loughgall H911519, Woodville J077597.

GAZETTEER OF CASTLES IN COUNTY CAVAN

CLOGHOUGHTER   H358078   D

The de Lacys are thought to have built this circular tower upon a crannog in Lough Oughter in the early 13th century but it soon fell to the O'Reillys. The Irish Confederate Catholics imprisoned Bishop Bedell in the castle in 1641, and Eoghan Rua O'Neill died here in 1649. Apart from the south side, which was destroyed after the castle was captured by Cromwellian troops in 1653, the tower stands 18m high and is 15.5m in diameter over walls 2.5m thick. The lowest level was subdivided by a crosswall in the 17th century and has two original loops and part of a later doorway. Beam-holes remain for the floor above, where there remain the original entrance, evidence of two windows, and doorways to the wall-walk of a lost curtain wall and an adjoining latrine turret. The third storey has windows of the early 17th century, when the castle was leased to the Culme family. They erected a new L-planned house on the shore 200m to the SE at Inishconnell but it and the outer earthworks built to defend it in the 1640s have been levelled. See page 5.

CROVER   N471854

On a rocky island in Lough Sheelin are overgrown remains of a tower built in the late 14th century by Thomas McMahon O'Reilly. It measures 10m by 8.5m over walls 2m thick above a battered base and has traces of a vault over the lowest storey, where there was an entrance in the south wall. From it a stair rose up in the east wall. There is a latrine chute on the north side.

PORT ISLAND   H033390

Hidden amongst dense vegetation on an island in Lough Macnean are the battered lower part of a ashlar-faced tower about 9.6m in diameter over walls 1.4m thick and several other small rectangular buildings. This may be the castle of "Inisochta" where Con O'Rourke imprisoned Malaghlin MacRannall in 1499.

TONYMORE   H397031

The west wall and most of the north wall are missing of this tower measuring 12.8m by 8.8m but parts of the south and east walls stand three storeys high. The latter is 4.5m thick and contained chambers over a central entrance passage with two drawbar slots and a murder-hole, and a spiral stair in the SE corner with its doorway off the passage also having a drawbar slot.

TULLYMONGAN   H421045

On a drumlin SE of Cavan stood an O'Reilly castle destroyed by the English in 1427 but rebuilt and shown on a map of 1591 as a tower with a west doorway and turrets on the NW and SE corners with a bawn enclosing several buildings. Vaults remained in the 19th century and earthworks still outlined a bawn about 29m square as recently as 1946.

Cloghoughter Castle

Plan of Crover Castle

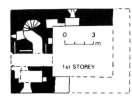

Plan of Tonymore Castle

OTHER CASTLE REMAINS IN COUNTY CAVAN

ASHGROVE H375133 18th century house said to incorporate massive 17th century lower parts. Fragment of possible thin bawn wall to west.

BAWN N368844 Damaged earthworks of bawn 75m by 60m

BAWNBOY H213196 D-shaped flanker about 7m across is only relic of house and bawn.

BALLYMAGAURAN H211133 Lowest two storeys of tower of c1600 about 12m by 9m with fireplace behind projecting east end of south wall. Damaged head on NW corner.

CABRA N790973 NE corner of ruined 18th century house incorporates part of castle built by Captain Gerald Fleming in 1607 and shown on Down Survey of c1656.

CASTLE COSBY H381011 Reset carved head on house. Yard contains southern part of circular SW corner flanker of castle known as Bunraskeen.

CASTLE RAHAN N535863 4m high ringwork 40m by 25m with traces of circular towers in NE and SW corners, the latter having footings of a building 11m by 7m near it.

FARNHAM H394060 House incorporates parts of building of c1610-20. SE corner flanker of bawn with upper storey vault seems to have survived until early 20th century.

LISSANOVER H234167 NE corner only of L-shaped building mostly destroyed in 1909.

POTTLE EAST H521138 Traces of 40m square bawn perhaps with NE corner flanker. The supposedly fortified house 16.5m square at Redhill is probably mid 18th century.

MOTTES (with baileys *): Knockatemple* N584857, Lavagh N442862, Moat N426844, Racraveen* N494864, Relagh* N690920, Stragehlin* H360169, Tanderagee N676962.

CASTLE SITES IN COUNTY CAVAN

BAILIEBOROUGH N662982 Site of house and bawn of the Cromwellian William Baillie.

BALLYCONNELL H275186 House of 1764 on site of bawn with two storey flankers and central three storey tower built c1610 by Captain Culme and Walter Talbot destroyed by accidental fire.

BELLANACARGY or CASTLE CARRICK H478111 Site of O'Reilly tower on rock. Surrounded by bawn 53m by 32m with entrance and corner flankers on south side.

CASTLE SAUNDERSON H418199 Later house on site of Captain Alexander Saunderson's house and bawn with two flankers destroyed during the war of 1689-91.

CLOGHBALLYBEG N674857 Site of O'Reilly tower beside Mullagh Lough built in 1486, remodelled by Sir William Taaffe c1610 and destroyed or abandoned in the 1650s.

CORDOAGH N747959 No remains of 15th century tower of Conor O'Reilly but three walls around a bawn 58m by 44m survived until early 20th century.

CORGREAGH H343192 Last remains of Sir Hugh Wirrall's house of 1618 have now gone. It was later occupied by Edward Bagshaw and then Thomas Richardson.

CORRANEARY or HANSBOROUGH H648058 Site of John Hamilton's house and bawn of c1613-20.

CROAGHAN H301085 Circular two storey SW flanker 4.5m in diameter of former bawn.

GRILLY H383179 Site of probable O'Reilly castle. Traces visible a century ago.

KEELAGH H318072 House of c1900 built from materials of older building on same site.

LISLIN H494117 Traces of platform 50m across beside house with battered base.

LISNAMAINE N340155 Site of John Fishe's house of 1611-13 built within a ringfort.

LURGANBOY Unlocated site of tower built by the Bradys probably in the 1580s. Rebuilt after its destruction in 1596 by Phillip O'Reilly.

MOYNEHALL H425023 Moulded corner bartizan base loose in yard SW corner.

RAHARDRUM N618866 Island 50m by 35m by shore of Lough Ramor may be site of a late 16th century O'Reilly castle. Evidence of ditch on landward side.

SHERCOCK H7210588 Chapel on supposed site of Sir Henry Piers' bawn and house.

SKEAGH H658015 Farm on site of William Hamilton's bawn with two flankers.

TULLYVIN H570097 Site of O'Reilly castle of c1450 later part of Moore Manor.

There were bawns at CASTLE POLES N306970 and KILLYFANA H422172. Other possible castle sites: Aghabane, Ballanghanea, Boagh, Cloone, Corlat, Drumcarn, Drumholme, Drumman, Drumshiel, Duffcastle, Dundavan, Knocknaveagh, Lisgannon, Lismore, Rantavan.

GAZETTEER OF CASTLES IN COUNTY DONEGAL

BALLYBOYLE   G905766

A shapeless fragment on a cliff edge is a relic of the "fair stone house" and bawn built by Paul Gore, to whom Ballyboyle was assigned after being granted to Patrick Vans in 1610. In 1601 the O'Boyles had their chief seat here, it having been recovered by Red Hugh O'Donnell from English forces which had occupied it since 1592. An O'Boyle castle here is first mentioned in 1440 when it was captured by one of the O'Donnells.

BALLYSHANNON   G879614

A barracks of c1700 stands on the site of an O'Donnell castle of 1423 north of the market place which commanded the lowest bridging point on the River Erne. In the rising of 1597 it successfully withstood an attack by an English force under Sir Conyers Clifford. James I reserved the castle to the Crown when Rory O'Donnell was created Earl of Tyrconnel in 1603. Lord Folliot later replaced it with a bawn.

BUNCRANA   C342326   D

On a low-lying site beside a stream is a tower measuring 9.8m by 8.7m with straight slab-roofed stairs in the north and east walls connecting three unvaulted storeys with all the lower openings now blocked up. The lower parts could be 14th century but the top storey and the parapets and harled gables date from 1602 when Hugh Boy O'Doherty refurbished the castle as a base for the Spanish troops expected in support of the Catholic rebellion against Elizabeth I. Her troops burnt the castle but it was repaired and in 1608 James I granted it to Sir Arthur Chichester. It was leased to the Vaughans who inserted large upper windows and fireplaces and lived in the tower until 1718, when Sir John Vaughan demolished the bawn wall to provide materials for the construction of a new mansion on the hill above.

Plan of Castle Bawn

1st STOREY   2nd STOREY

Plans of Burt Castle

1st STOREY

Buncrana: plan

Buncrana Castle

Burt Castle

Carrickabraghy

2ND STOREY

Doe: plan

Carrickabraghy Castle

BURT   G317193   D

The earliest mention of this castle is in a grant of land to Sir John Doherty in 1587 and it was then probably newly built. It was captured by Sir Henry Docwra in 1601 and is depicted on a map of that date as an embattled tower of three storeys plus an attic standing amidst several beehive huts within a square bawn flanked at diagonally opposite corners by casemates with musket loops. The bawn and its surrounding dry ditch has vanished but the tower stands almost to full height and measures 8.7m by 6.5m over walls 1.5m thick. There are turrets 3.2m in diameter at diagonally opposite corners. One contains the staircase adjacent to a tier of mural chambers over the destroyed entrance. There are gunloops but no vaults, except for those over the mural chambers. The castle was besieged by the English in 1607, taken during the rebellion of 1608 of Sir Cahir O'Doherty, and later granted to Thomas Chichester. See page 37.

CARRICKABRAGHY   C397524   C

A map of 1690 depicts here an oval bawn with seven flankers of which only slight traces now survive. Two unvaulted storeys remain of a central tower measuring just 5.6m by 5m externally with a stair leading up from the north side of the upper storey. There are only traces of an added third storey. Adjoining it are fragments of a round tower 5m in diameter with gunloops, beyond which is the bawn gateway with a drawbar slot. Part of another circular flanker remains 40m SSE of the tower house. It was here that Sir Cahir O'Doherty planned his revolt of 1608.

CASTLE BAWN   B923321   D

Low walls 1m thick enclose an overgrown wedge-shaped court 16m by 10m on a promontory bounded by the sea and a stream in a gorge. The north wall stands higher and has a gateway with a drawbar slot and a narrow staircase. Lands granted in 1611 to Henry Hart were sold to Wybrant Olphert, who possessed here a "stone fort" by 1619.

DOE   C085318   E

This is the most complete of the tower-and-bawn type castles of the native Irish chiefs of Ulster. The Quins are thought to have built the central tower, which measures 9.2m by 7.6m over walls 1.6m thick and rises through four unvaulted storeys to a level wall-head 16.5m above ground. A recent roof has replaced the former gabled attic room. There are stairs in the east wall and latrines on the north side. The tower is first mentioned in 1544 in connection with the struggles between the sons of MacSweeney of Tuatha. This family added the narrow building extending round the south and east sides of the tower with a beehive slab-roofed casement with gunloops set at its NE corner and a larger and more altered flanking tower also with gunloops at the SW corner. An apartment 10m long by 5.7m wide extends south out to the wall 1.3m thick surrounding a bawn 31m by 27m around the tower. The wall-walk is reached by steps on the north and east sides and has machicolations over the gateway facing the sea on the east and on the south side, and on three of the corners, whilst the NE corner has a boldly projecting and steeply battered flanker bristling with gunloops. There is also a projection at a change of alignment on the south side and a turret on the west side, beside which is a later entrance with a barbican with gunloops extending over the dry moat defending the landward side.

The castle was taken over for the English Crown c1600 by Eoghan Og MacSweeney. He resisted attacks by his brother Rory and Red Hugh O'Donnell. The castle was granted to Rory O'Donnell c1603 but was recaptured by the MacSweeneys in 1606. Sir Cahir O'Doherty took the castle in 1608 and used it as a base for an attack on Derry. The MacSweeneys were back in possession from 1641 until Sir Charles Coote captured the castle in a surprise attack in 1650. Colonel Myles MacSweeney was defeated by Coote after he weakened his Catholic army by detaching 1,400 men from it in an attempt to recapture the castle. A royal garrison was maintained at Doe during Charles II's reign but the MacSweeneys captured it in support of James II in 1689 only to be dispossessed soon afterwards. The castle lay ruinous during the 18th century but in the early 1800s was restored as a residence for Captain George Vaughan Harte, whose arms appear over the inner doorway. Many of the features of the tower and the adjoining block, and parts of the bawn wall, particularly the parapet, date from this period. The castle was finally abandoned c1900.

Doe Castle

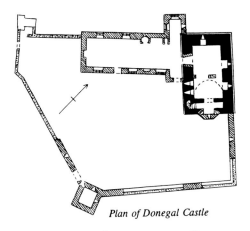

Plan of Donegal Castle

0   20
metres

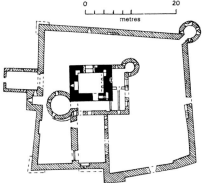

Plan of Doe Castle

Flanker at Doe

Casemate at Doe

Donegal Castle

Donegal Castle

DONEGAL   G930786   E

Donegal was the chief seat of the O'Donnells of Tyrconnell. Hugh O'Donnell and Nuala O'Brien are thought to have begun the tower house in the 1470s. It measures 16.6m by 10.6m over walls 2.3m thick and has a vaulted basement formerly entered through a lobby in the extra thick SE wall which also contains a spiral staircase. Of the 1560s are the doorway with ferns in the spandrels of the four-centred arch leading from the stair to the hall above, and a fireplace with similar motifs. In 1591 the English occupied Donegal and fortified the friary, and in 1595 Red Hugh O'Donnell is said to have burnt his own castle here to prevent the English occupying it. In 1602 Red Hugh's cousin Niall Garbh held the friary for the English until its magazine exploded and wrecked the building.

James I recognised Red Hugh as Earl of Tyrconnell in 1603 but Hugh found his position here untenable and in 1607 he fled into exile in Spain. Sir Basil Brooke was then granted the friary and in 1616 he was given a lease (and later outright ownership) of the town and the derelict castle. He remodelled the upper parts of the tower house, providing the two upper storeys with mullion-and-transom windows and an attic with more such windows in numerous gables. There are two boldly projecting square turrets on the corners at the SE end, where a bay was built up in front of the original doorway to provide a three-sided window in the end wall of the hall which has a fireplace with the arms of Sir Basil (who died in 1633) and his wife Anne Leycester. A new doorway connected the tower with a new wing extending to the SW with further mullioned windows and five cross-gables. This wing contains a new main entrance, beside which was a kitchen, whilst a wing at the back facing NW contained a staircase. A reset upper doorway is probably from the friary. The fragmentary wall enclosing a bawn 45m by 37m is also mostly of this period, and has a diagonally projecting square tower beside the south facing gateway, although a fragment at the west corner could be a remnant of an older bawn. The Brookes supported Parliament in the wars of the 1640s and in 1651 the Marquis of Clanricard took the castle and briefly tried to hold it against the Cromwellians. The Irish Board of Works has re-roofed the tower house and one bay of the adjoining wing during the 1990s, almost a century after the ruins was first taken into state guardianship. See plan on page 29.

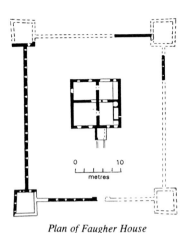

Plan of Faugher House

Inch Castle

FAUGHER or WRAY   C053362 D

Tirlough Oge O'Boyle's bawn of c1611 was confiscated in the 1650s and given to Sir John Stephens and Hugh Hamill. Originally known as Faugher House, it was renamed Wray Castle after being sold in 1700 to William Wray. A square thinly-walled mid or late 17th century house subdivided by crosswalls into four rooms of unequal size on each of three low storeys with part of a porch remaining on the south side lies in the middle of a rectangular bawn 24m by 29m, enclosed by a loopholed wall 0.7m thick and 2.9m high. The wall is fragmentary except for the complete SW side and little remains of the four rectangular corner flankers each measuring about 5.5m by 5m with acute outermost angles. One jamb with a drawbar slot remains of the gateway on the SE side.

FORT STEWART   C274202

The only remains of the wall up to 1.3m thick around a kite-shaped bawn about 21m across built by Sir William Stewart c1619 are short lengths adjoining the two surviving flankers with gunloops and parapets, that at the SE corner being circular and 4.5m in diameter, whilst that at the NW corner (adjoining a jamb of the west facing gateway with a drawbar slot) is larger and spear-head shaped.

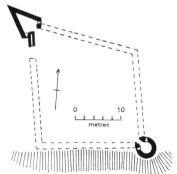

Plan of Fort Stewart

Faugher House

Greencastle

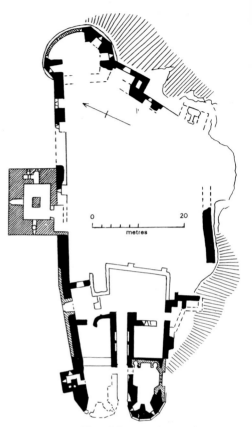

Plan of Greencastle

GREENCASTLE   C654403   A

This building, also called Northburg or Newcastle, was begun in 1305 by Richard de Burgh, Earl of Ulster to subdue the neighbouring O'Neills and O'Donnells. In 1316 it was captured by King Robert of Scotland's younger brother Edward Bruce. He was killed after being crowned King of Ireland and the castle was recovered by the Earl. Richard's grandson William captured his kinsman Walter Burke in 1332 and starved him to death in the castle. In revenge the Burkes murdered Earl William at Belfast in 1333. The earl had no direct heir and English influence in Ulster immediately declined. Eventually the O'Dohertys took over Greencastle and in the 15th century added a large tower house which greatly strengthened the previously poorly flanked northern side.

In 1555 the castle was wrecked by Calbhach O'Donnell who ravaged the Inishowen peninsular with Scottish auxiliary troops after quarrelling with his father. It was not properly repaired until after 1608 when the castle was captured from the O'Dohertys and granted to Sir Arthur Chichester. It was garrisoned until at least the 1690s and in 1812 a new fort further east took over its role of guarding the narrow entrance of Lough Foyle.

The castle has an irregularly shaped court 30m wide protected by cliffs to the south and east. It extends 59m eastwards from the back of a gatehouse with twin polygonal fronted towers to the straight inner wall (now only footings) of a large polygonal NE tower of irregular plan. A square latrine turret lies on the north side of the gatehouse and there is another (now very fragmentary) at the SE corner of the court. The gatehouse contained the main apartments and had behind it service rooms and a small lower court. In the 17th century a new kitchen was created in the room flanking the south side of the entrance passage, which has a vaulted basement below it, and a low parapet replaced a part of the outer wall of the NW tower which had fallen or been dismantled. The tower house built over and against the north curtain wall facing flat ground measures 14m by 13m over walls 3.3m thick. There is a large central pier to help support the floor of the upper storey which has embrasures giving access to a latrine and a well.

INCH C322223

On a rock on the south side of Inch island stands the east half of a tower and footings of a bawn built in the 1430s by Neachtan O'Donnell with the consent of his father-in-law O'Doherty of Inishowen. In 1454 the Tyrconnell lordship was disputed by two O'Donnell cousins, one whom, Donnell, was imprisoned by O'Doherty in the castle. The other cousin, Rory, was killed by a stone thrown from the battlements whilst leading an attack upon the castle. Donnell thus became lord of Tyrconnell but was killed by Rory's brother Turlough in 1456. The castle was already ruinous by 1600 when the English devastated the island and it does not seem to have been restored. It is 9.8m wide and was about 14m long over walls 2.1m thick. A crosswall divided the lower part into two cellars with lofts under the vaults. A straight stair in the north wall led up from the entrance to a doorway in the NE corner of the hall over the vaults and then continued up in the east wall. The hall has a latrine in the SE corner. See photo on page 31.

KILBARRON G837652 G

On a sheer-sided 15m high coastal promontory are remains of an irregularly shaped bawn 45m long by 33m wide entered through the southern part of the lowest level of a tower house 16.5m long by 11m wide over walls 1.7m thick now nowhere more than 2m high. This tower occupies the northern half of the east side, where the site is protected by a ditch. The rest of the basement was further subdivided and there is a projecting latrine turret at the NW corner. There are fragments of other buildings in the bawn SE and SW corners. The castle was built in the 15th century by the O'Sgingins, hereditary historiographers of Tyrconnell. Both office and castle later passed to the O'Clerys, of which the most famous was Michael, main author the Annals of the Four Masters, born here in 1580. It was ruined before the 1650s, when it was held by Francis Brassy.

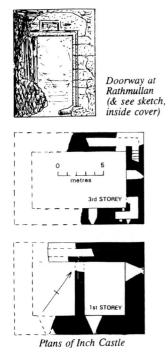

Doorway at Rathmullan (& see sketch, inside cover)

Plan of Kilbarron Castle

3rd STOREY

1st STOREY

Plans of Inch Castle

Kilbarron Castle

LIFFORD   C400980

The castle in which Red Hugh O'Donnell entertained an ambassador sent by Philip II of Spain in 1596 was replaced by a "good strong fort of lime and stone" begun in 1611 by Sir Richard Hansard. An early 17th century survey shows a fort with angle bastions at diagonally opposite corners lying at one corner of the roughly triangular town defences of the same period. Nothing remains of any of these works, although Sir Richard's fine tomb of c1620 survives in the Protestant parish church.

LOUGH ESKE   G972825

This castle was a major O'Donnell seat until captured by Sir Henry Folliott during the rebellion of Sir Cahir O'Doherty in 1608. Walls 2m thick and up to 3m high enclose a bawn 39m by 35m now completely choked by vegetation. There are three embrasures on the west side, a fourth facing east near the SE corner and a fifth with gunloops in the middle of the south side. The badly ruined north side has a central gateway and what appears to be a passage giving access to a boat-shed built against the outer wall. There may have been a tower on the promontory beyond it. A sheila-na-gig removed from the ruins to the coach-house of the house of 1859-61 has now disappeared. The yard of this house has a datestone of 1621 with initials W.H. and I.M., there having been a 17th century house here once. Hidden under ivy and vegetation by the shore nearby (at 961825) are the 1m thick west wall up to 7m high and part of the north wall of a tower of c1600 about 8.4m by 8m containing two vaulted cellars divided by a crosswall with a vaulted passage on the south probably connecting them with stairs in the SE corner.

MONGAVLIN   C350065

A rectangular stronghouse 15m long by 7.4m wide built by Sir John Stewart c1620 was used by James II as a base during the siege of Derry. It remained inhabited until the mid 19th century but only the two end walls 1.2m thick now remain. They have Scottish type corbelling for three of the circular corner bartizans and various fireplaces, the south end having a private room over a kitchen whilst the northern part had a hall over offices or cellars. There were bedrooms on the third storey and servants' rooms in the roof. The lower windows have the marks or former protective iron grilles, another Scottish feature. The entrance lay in the middle of the east side.

Raphoe Palace

Mongavlin Castle

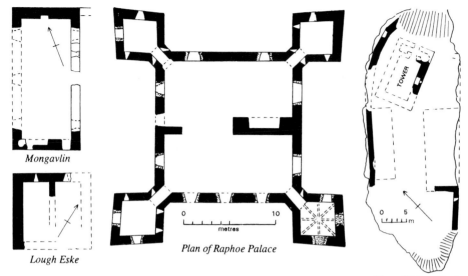

Mongavlin

Lough Eske

Plan of Raphoe Palace

Plan of Rahan Castle

MOROSS   C182388

On the north side of a small rocky island connected to the shore by a 45m long causeway is a 6m high fragment of the SW corner of a tower containing a passage in the west facing wall 2.4m thick. Built in 1532 by the McSwynes, the castle was inhabited in 1601 by Alexander McDonaloghe and in 1610 was granted to Henry Vaughan. It was leased to Arthur Terry but later abandoned when he moved to Derry.

RAHAN   G754645

This castle is first mentioned in 1524 and in 1601 was described as the chief seat of McSwyne Bannagh. In 1622 it was occupied by Herbert Maxwell as a tenant of John Murray, Earl of Annandale, and had recently been given a new gatehouse, although some parts were then ruined. A promontory with cliffs on three sides and a ditch on the eastern landward side bears fragments on the north and SW of a wall up to 1.5m thick around a court 45m long by 21m wide. There are signs of buildings along the long sides and the NE end was filled by a tower house 13.5m by 9.8m. Of it there remain footings of the east wall containing the entrance and a 10m high fragment of the south wall with evidence of a spiral stair in the SE corner and a vault over the third storey.

RAPHOE   C259028   G

Bishop John Leslie's palace of 1636-7 is a block 16m square with a partly destroyed central spine wall thickened to contain a huge kitchen fireplace in the low basement partly below ground. There are gunloops in the boldly projecting corner towers which are almost square internally but with acute outermost corners. The palace was besieged by the rebel Irish in 1641, captured by Cromwellian forces in 1650, and plundered by James II's troops in 1688. Large new windows were inserted in the mid 18th century and a brick vault was inserted into the base of one of the towers to create a strongroom or ice-house. The last bishop, William Bisset, added the embattled fourth storey with bartizans on the outermost corners. Shortly after the Protestant diocese was united with that of Derry in 1835 and the palace became redundant it was burnt down by a prospective tenant in the hope of obtaining a cheaper lease on the lands.

RATHMULLAN   C292276   A

A 16th century military map shows to the SW of the friary a now-vanished MacSwyne castle which had been captured by the O'Donnells in 1516. Red Hugh O'Donnell was captured here in 1587 when he was lured aboard an English ship to sample some wines. In 1603 the friary was granted by James I to Sir James Fullerton, who allowed Sir Ralph Bingley to use it as a barracks. In 1617 the friary was obtained by Andrew Knox, Protestant Bishop of Raphoe, and the nave and south transept of the church were then converted into an L-shaped three storey stronghouse, round bartizans of Scottish type with moulded corbelling being added to the nave west gable, whilst the cloister became a bawn. The east end was retained unaltered as a chapel and the thin original central tower still divides off that part. A new projection between the nave and transept contained a wooden scale-and-platt staircase. This part contains the entrance covered by a machicolation and surmounted by a stone with the date 1618 and the bishop's initials.

TERMON   G096653   D

This castle was built c1615 by James MacGrath, son of a Catholic Bishop of Down who adopted Protestantism in 1567 and held the archbishopric of Cashel from 1571 until 1603. It has been a ruin since Colonel Henry Ireton demolished much of the landward-facing northern sides of the tower and bawn with cannonfire during a siege in 1650. The tower measures 11.7m by 9.4m over steeply battered walls 2m thick at the base. A circular NE corner turret contains a stair connecting the three upper storeys, the topmost two of which have windows of two and three lights and were connected by a second stair in the NW corner. The turret base is solid and access from the east-facing entrance to the foot of the stair must have been via a wooden stair or ladder within the low basement, which was lighted by five loops, there being no vaulting. At the summit are square machicolated bartizans on the southern corners and the remains of stepped merlons. The 27m wide bawn extends 19m north of the tower, the eastern side extending down to enclose the tower doorway. The loopholed wall is 0.9m thick and has a fireplace of an outbuilding on the west side and circular flankers 4m in diameter at the NE and NW corners. See cover.

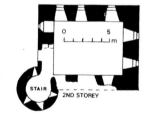

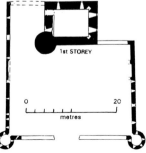

Termon Castle   *Plans of Termon Castle*

OTHER CASTLE REMAINS IN COUNTY DONEGAL

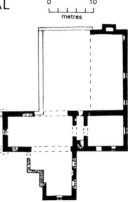

0   10
metres

ARDLANDS Small fragment on island in Castle Port Bay.
CASTLE STUKE C421518 Traces of O'Doherty refuge
    tower on low coastal stack.
DUNOWEN Double promontory on Inishowen cut off by
    drystone wall. Site of castle held in 1601 by Gartell, son
    of Sean Buidhe O'Doherty.
KILTOURISLOUGH G681967 2m thick and 3.5m high
    fragment with mural stair of castle on island with
    causeway to shore. Occupied by Bishop O'Boyle in 1601.
RAMELTON C228213 Modern building may incorporate
    parts of Sir William Stewart's three storey tower with a
    staircase turret, bartizans, and bawn erected c1610-20.
STONEWOLD G899609 2m high base of tower 11m by
    8.5m over walls 2m thick upon mound submerged by
    River Erne hydro-electric scheme.

Plan of Rathmullan Friary

CASTLE SITES IN COUNTY DONEGAL

ARDAHEE C131097 O'Donnell tower by River Swilly demolished in early 19th century.
BALLYMAGROARTY G902687 Part of 15m long building still survived in 1847.
CARRIGANS Unlocated site of O'Donnell castle sold by Arthur Chichester to Sir Ralph
    Bingley in 1610.
CASTLE FINN H263946 Site of O'Donnell tower by ford remodelled and given an
    adjoining bawn c1610-20 by Sir John Kingsmill, but ruinous by the mid 1650s.
CULMACATRAINE C325174 Castle Forward lies on or near site of O'Doherty castle
    dismantled in 1529, but later occupied by O'Donnells and occupied by English in 1610.
DRUMDUTTON C111326 Site of stronghouse of Captain Thomas Dutton burnt during
    the wars of the 1640s. Shed east of church built against fragment of uncertain date.
DUNALONG Unlocated site of tower and bawn built in 1568 by Turlough Luineach
    O'Neill. Surrounded c1601 by pentagonal earthwork town defences with angle
    bastions but soon abandoned.
FAHAN C349253 Site of castle dismantled in 1600. Ogival-headed window with sunk
    spandrels found during demolition work at Castletown House in mid 20th century.
KILLYBEGS G713759 Site of bawn 18m square later replaced by harbour battery.
KILLYGORDON H207936 Site of Captain Ralph Mansfield's house and bawn of 1610-22.
KILLYNURE C090005 House on site of William Wilson's house and bawn of c1610-22.
KILNACRENAN C146207 Slight traces on probable
    site of Captain William Stewart's house.
LIFFORD Sir Richard Hansard's "good strong fort"
    replaced an O'Donnell tower.
RED CASTLE C561348 Site of castle held by
    Hugh Carrogh McLaughlin in 1601 and captured
    by English in 1608. Later held by Sir Richard
    Hansard as a tenant of the Chichesters.
WHITECASTLE C528327 Late 18th century house
    on or near site of building occupied in 1601 by
    Brian Oge McLaughlin. Held in 1654 by Major
    George Carey as a tenant of Lord Chichester.
OTHER CASTLE SITES: Bundrowes G792582,
    Castleross C302380, Cavan Lower
    H177953, Doaghcrabbin C244420, Dunfanaghy
    C028374, Woodhill C037365.

Old sketch of Burt Castle

GAZETTEER OF CASTLES IN COUNTY DOWN

ARDGLASS   J560371   E & C

By the shore are remains of an embattled medieval warehouse 65m long called the Newark or Horn Castle which seems to have been divided into three units with offices or domestic accommodation at the east end. The western part is incorporated in an 18th century house now used as a golf clubhouse. Near it are three urban tower houses, a fourth known as King's Castle having been destroyed not long after it was rebuilt in the 19th century. The best preserved of the three towers takes its name from the Jordan family, one of whom, Simon, was blockaded here by the O'Neills for three years until relieved by Lord Mountjoy in June 1601. Probably built in the early 15th century, it measures 8m by 6.5m and has two turrets on the north side. The widest one contains the spiral stair with the entrance at its foot equipped with a drawbar slot and covered by a machicolation high up, where an arch joins the turrets and has a second machicolation slot behind it and at right-angles to the other one. Over a vaulted cellar with three double-splayed loops is a hall with a fireplace, two windows with seats in the embrasures, and a latrine in the narrower NE turret. There are two further similar rooms above, although the fourth storey had neither a fireplace or latrine. This building was restored from ruin by the antiquarian Francis Joseph Biggar after his purchase of it in 1911, and it has been a monument in State car since his death in 1926. Nearby (at 560371) is the similarly planned Margaret's Castle where the main block measures 6.8m by 6.6m and the entrance lies in the main north wall rather than in the base of the stair turret. It now lacks its upper parts. Between it and the warehouse is Cowd's Castle, a plain tower without turrets measuring just 5.8m by 5.4m.

Audleys: plans of tower house

Plan of Audley's Castle

Jordan's Castle, Ardglass

Audleys; section

Plan of Jordan's Castle at Ardglass

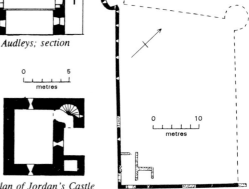

Plan of Ballydugan Castle

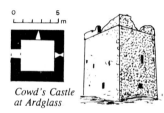

*Cowd's Castle
at Ardglass*

AUDLEY'S   J578506   E

The Audleys had their seat here until they sold it to their neighbour Bernard Ward in 1646. The 15th century tower stands on or near the site of a motte and lies in the north corner of a bawn 28m by 20m within a wall 1m thick now reduced to its lowest courses. There are traces of buildings including a fireplace along the NE side of the bawn. The tower measures 9.1m by 7.7m and contained a vaulted hall above a basement with double-splayed loops, plus a private room on top, and it rises 11m to the top of the parapet. Turrets projecting 2m towards the court contain the spiral staircase and latrines for the upper two levels. Joining the turrets at the top is an arch with a machicolation behind it to protect the doorway at the foot of the stair. The turret tops are missing but a third turret on the west corner remains intact.

Embattled warehouse at Ardglass

BALLYDUGAN   J468431

An account of 1744 describes the burning of a bawn here in 1641 as a result of the treachery of Irish servants. The bawn measured 38m by 26m and still retains walls 3m high on the SE and SW sides, the latter having several gunloops. Part of the 5m diameter west corner flanker, circular externally but with two storeys of polygonal rooms internally, also remains.

BANGOR   J505822   C

On the waterfront is a customs house built in 1637 by Sir James Hamilton, 1st Viscount Clandeboye. The main block 16m by 8.3m has storey storeys and an attic within a roof with crowstepped gables in the Scottish manner. At one corner a round tower contains a stair from the entrance to the upper storey. Above the stair is a room reached by a stair in a turret corbelled out over a re-entrant angle.

Audley's Castle

Castle Bright: plan

0   5
L__I__I__I__I__J m

3rd STOREY

2nd STOREY

Castle Ward   *Castle Bright*

Castle Ward: plans

CASTLE BRIGHT   J506382   C

The east end wall of a tower 6.2m wide probably built by the Russell family c1600-10 stands to the full height of 8.4m to a wall-walk above three low storeys. The lowest level has three double-splayed loops and was intended to have a vault, but if built it must have been fairly flat in section. The window embrasures above had timber-lintels.

CASTLE REAGH   J375711

A Presbyterian church on the SE edge of Belfast is thought to stand near the site of the former main seat of the Clannoboy O'Neills. It was sold in 1616 to Sir Moses Hill, who added flankers to the bawn, and was dismantled in 1809.

CASTLE WARD   J574498   C

Amongst the service buildings of an 18th century mansion now administered by the National Trust is a tower built in 1610 by Nicholas Ward, a Cheshire man who obtained a government position in Ireland at the end of Elizabeth I's reign. It measures 8.8m by 7.8m and rises almost 14m to the top of the double-stepped battlements. A brick arch has been made in the south end of the vaulted lowest storey. Straight stairs in the east and south walls lead up to the hall and bedroom. Both have two-light windows over where there is an entrance doorway at the foot of the stairs. It is protected by a machicolation from the parapet and has a stipple decoration of a type more common in Munster and Connacht.

CLOUGH   J409403   A

This fine motte has a ditch with a counterscarp and a bailey platform to the south measuring 34m by 20m. The 24m diameter motte summit has a tiny two storey 13th century tower just 6.8m by 4.1m over walls 0.9m thick on the west side and slight traces of a central hall block with clasping corner buttresses. In the 17th century the tower was given a wing projecting 3.4m with two double-splayed loops. Coins of King John's reign and pits for archers were found on the motte summit during excavations.

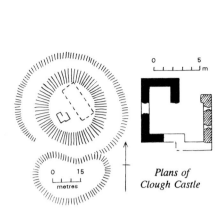

Plans of
Clough Castle

Clough Castle

DOWNPATRICK   J482450 A

In 1177 John de Courcy captured the seat here of Rory MacDonlevy, King of Ulster in a surprise attack. An attempt to recapture the place was crushed with heavy losses to the native Irish. The large pear-shaped enclosure 165m by 120m with a huge rampart on the vulnerable SE must represent the original Irish fort whilst the large and apparently unfinished motte within it must be the work of de Courcy.

DROMORE   J202532 C & 206532 A

On a rise to the SE of the cathedral is a three storey tower about 8.5m square with a damaged wing in the middle of the east side which probably contained the entrance and staircase. The upper storeys have centrally placed windows and narrow gunloops near the corners. The tower was built c1610 by William Worsley on land leased from his brother-in-law Bishop John Todd. Further east is a very fine motte rising 12m above its ditch to a summit 18m by 16m lying on the north side of a 30m square bailey platform above the River Lagan. The motte has a large counterscarp bank beyond its ditch. See page 5.

Motte and bailey castle at Dromore

Dundrum Castle

DUNDRUM   J404370   A

The 1m thick wall of the oval upper ward 56m by 40m was probably built in the 1190s by John de Courcy. He was dispossessed by Hugh de Lacy in 1204 and failed to recover the castle by force in 1205. King John took over the castle in 1210. The 14m high four storey circular keep 14.6m in diameter over walls 2m thick above the battered plinth probably dates from after 1227, when Henry III granted the castle to Hugh de Lacy, Earl of Ulster. The original entrance was at second storey level but a new entrance was made at ground level beside the foot of the spiral stair in the 15th century, when the topmost storey was also remodelled. Expenditure recorded in the 1260s may refer to the building of the gatehouse. It has square guard rooms on either side of a central passage, but in front of the east part was a semi-circular tower, the only part to project beyond the curtain wall, and now reduced to its base. The approach at an oblique angle from the west round the side of the rock prevented the provision of the usual second such tower.

The wall of the outer bailey extending down the hillside for 67m to the SE is thin except on the vulnerable west side, where it has its own separate entrance. It could be of any period from the 13th century onwards. The castle was said to be ruinous in 1333 and was taken over by the Magennises, a native Irish family. Lord Grey captured the castle from them in 1538 and Felim Magennis surrendered it to the Crown in 1610. A new L-shaped house was built in the SW corner of the outer ward after the castle was granted to Sir Francis Blundell in 1636. The Magennises recovered the castle during the revolt of 1641 but it was captured and slighted by the Cromwellians in 1652.

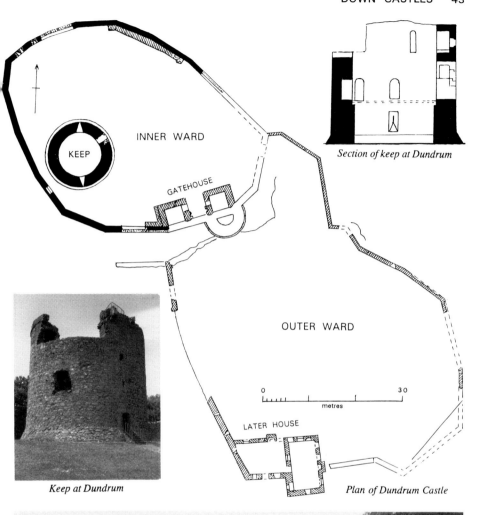

INNER WARD

KEEP

GATEHOUSE

Section of keep at Dundrum

OUTER WARD

0   30

metres

LATER HOUSE

Keep at Dundrum

Plan of Dundrum Castle

Upper ward at Dundrum

GREENCASTLE   J247118   A

The mound of the timber earliest castle here lies near the end of the peninsular. The keep was built by Henry III in the 1230s and was repaired in 1252 and again in 1260 after being wrecked by the Irish. It was then surrounded by a walled court 47m by 37m with U-shaped corner towers and a rock-cut ditch on the east side. The Crown entrusted the castle to the Earls of Ulster and it was the original home of Elizabeth de Burgh, second wife of Robert Bruce, King of Scotland, whose brother Edward captured and sacked the castle in 1316. It was vulnerable to Irish attacks after the murder of Earl William in 1333. Six catapults were sent to help stiffen the defences in 1335 when the castle had to be relieved twice by Henry de Maundeville from besieging Irish forces. It was stormed and wrecked in 1343 but soon repaired, only to be again wrecked in 1375 by the Magennises of Iveagh. In 1408 John More lost his office as constable of the castles of Greencastle and Carlingford because he had failed to keep them properly repaired or garrisoned. The Earls of Kildare were keepers from 1505 until their downfall in 1534. Then and again in 1549 both castles were reported to be ruinous, but in 1552 Greencastle was granted to Sir Nicholas Bagenall, who is assumed to have inserted the large windows in the keep.

The whole of the SE corner tower and most of the adjacent walls have vanished and only fragments and foundations partly muddled up with farm buildings remain of the rest of the outer defences, whilst there is no sign of a gateway. One outbuilding south of the keep remains roofed but has been much altered. Another building lay on the north side and the north end of a third remains on the east side adjacent to the inner parts of the NE tower which include a latrine passage. The keep survives almost complete and measures 21.3m by 11.9m over walls 1.8m thick. The lowest storey was originally a dark single room reached only from the hall above but in the 16th century it was given crosswalls supporting vaults, double-splayed loops, and a new entrance in the west end wall with an internal stair rising beside it. The hall probably had a private room divided off at the east end where there is a latrine in a corner. The fireplace and the wide window embrasures are all 16th century. A spiral stair beside the original west-facing upper entrance rises to the battlements, where the clasping corner buttresses are continued up as turrets.

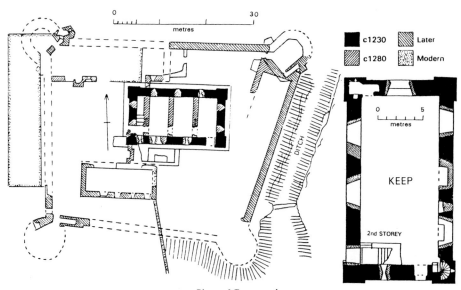

Plans of Greencastle

Greencastle

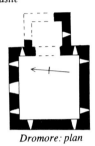

Kilclief: plan   *Dromore: plan*

Kilclief Castle

HILLHALL   J301644

Peter Hill is thought to have built this bawn in the 1630s after he purchased the estate then known as Kilmuck from Sir Robert McClelland. A wall 0.9m thick surrounds a court 60m by 42m and has a parapet and a very narrow wall-walk which must have had a timber platform built onto it. An account of 1744 mentions four corner flankers but the east and south corners are now missing, a T-shaped house occupies the north corner, and only the inner part remains of the west flanker, which measured about 4.5m in diameter. The entrance lies near the middle of the NW side.

HILLSBOROUGH   J245586   E

The fort erected by Peter Hill c1630 on the site of a rath was destroyed by the Irish in 1641 but it was rebuilt by his uncle and heir Colonel Arthur Hill, who renamed the place Hillsborough. At the restoration of 1660 it was made a royal garrison with Hill and his heirs as hereditary constables. William III stayed in the fort during his campaign of 1690. A square structure 80m across with a stone faced earth rampart with angled corner bastions, it seems to be 18th century in its present form. The gatehouse with four corner turrets on the NW side dates from 1758. By then the Hills had a house elsewhere.

KILCLIEF   J597457   B

This four storey tower measuring 10.2m by 8m existed by 1441 when John Cely, Bishop of Down, was dismissed from office for living here with his mistress. Projecting from the east wall are two turrets containing respectively the spiral stair with the entrance at its foot and a tier of latrines. At the top they are united by an arch with a machicolation behind it, above which the turret tops have been rebuilt. The west corners are also carried up as turrets and the upper storeys have chimney breasts corbelled out of the outer walls and two-light windows.

Narrow Water Castle

Killyleagh Castle

KILLYLEAGH   J523529   C

The Mandevilles held Killyleagh from c1330 until ousted by the Clannaboy O'Neills in the 16th century. In 1561 Elizabeth I granted the barony of Dufferin to the Whytes of Dublin. They sold Killyleagh in 1610 to Sir James Hamilton, Lord Clandeboye, who then built the core of the present building with a 7m diameter tower projecting from the south corner. It seems to have measured about 14m by 11.5m and the thick walls suggest the survival of earlier work although the evidence has been destroyed by refacing and rebuilding in 1850. To the latter period belong the mullioned windows and all the other existing details including the picturesque roofline with conical roofs on the towers and a parapet in front of three gables on the SE side. The main block contains several vaulted cellars and was badly damaged in 1648 when it was besieged and taken by General Monck for Cromwell. In a restoration of the castle in the 1660s by Henry Hamilton, 2nd Earl of Clanbrassil the main block was extended 4.5m to the NE and given a second tower 7.5m in diameter on the east corner, whilst large new bawn 90m long by 43m wide was laid out to the SE. The bawn entrance front was rebuilt in 1862 with a new central gatehouse. The pair of four storey corner flankers 5m square with spiral stairs in round turrets where they join the main wall are 17th century work, although a passage was forced through the east flanker at some later period. Both the flankers and their stair turrets and the merlons of the bawn wall-walk parapet contain gunloops and the east flanker bears the date 1666. In the rebuilt section of wall between the main block south tower and the turret at the west corner of the bawn is a reset doorway dated 1625. See page 9.

KIRKISTOWN   J645580

Roland Savage built this tower measuring 9.5m by 8.3m in 1622. The SE wall is 2.7m thick and contains a tier of chambers over the entrance flanked by a guard room on one side and a spiral staircase in the south corner. This wall has four habitable levels corresponding to three in the tower interior, the third of these being level with a vault over the main second storey room. There are well-preserved double stepped battlements with a machicolation over the entrance and the west corner raised up as a turret. Originally there was probably an attic within the battlements. The main windows date from a remodelling c1800 but a number of small original loops remain, including some with ogival heads. The porch and buttresses on the SE side also date from c1800 when the lowest part of the stair was replaced by two straight flights of steps. The tower lies within a bawn 43m wide and perhaps up to 76m long, although the position of the original NE wall is uncertain. The 0.9m thick wall has no foundations and has needed buttressing on the SW side, the best preserved part with one jamb of the gateway, several gunloops and others in the 5m diameter flankers at either end.

NARROW WATER   J125194 C

This castle protecting the long narrow arm of Carlingford Lough is thought to have been built by the English c1560, although it soon passed to the Magennises of Iveagh. After the war of 1689-91 it was confiscated and given to the Halls. It was used for industrial purposes during the 18th century. The tower measuring 11.2m by 10.1m over walls 2m thick contains three storeys and an attic within a wall-walk fitted with a box-machicolation over the west-facing entrance. It lies within a bawn about 36m across enclosed by a partly restored and rebuilt wall 0.6m thick rising 2m above the ground inside but rather more on the outside, where it rises directly from the rocky shore. The wall has a projection facing south towards the lough and a modern gateway towards the adjacent road on the north side. The tower contains a cellar with double-splayed loops and one other poorly lighted room under a vault and a third storey above with chambers in the NW and SE corners and four modified windows. Both upper levels have latrines in the SW corner. The NW corner is continued up as a turret above the main parapet.

NENDRUM or MAHEE   J524639 A

A tower 12.8m by 6.7m built in 1570 by Captain Browne guards the causeway approach to Mahee Island. The lowest level contained a cellar vaulted longitudinally with an entrance with a drawbar-slot at the NW end. There is also a smaller chamber vaulted in the other direction which was either a boat-house or a gateway passage onto the island. The cellar has remains of a stair up to the hall and a second stair in the diagonally opposite corner led to a third storey probably divided into two bedrooms. The south corner and parts of the adjoining sides have fallen.

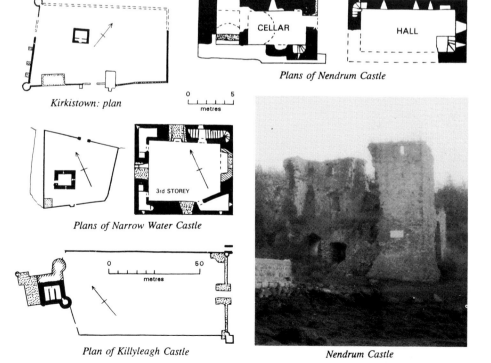

Plans of Nendrum Castle

Kirkistown: plan

Plans of Narrow Water Castle

Plan of Killyleagh Castle

Nendrum Castle

NEWRY   J087261

Old drawings in the Public Record Office in London depict a four storey tower built at Newry by Sir Nicholas Bagnall c1578. It had a wing adjoining one side and that end of the main block had a vaulted basement whilst the other end had a large kitchen fireplace with an entrance adjoining it. There was another entrance at the foot of a spiral stair in a turret in the middle of the other side. The upper storeys were also probably subdivided, but with timber partitions. Nothing is known of a castle said to have been built by the English authorities at Newry in 1480, or of a still earlier castle in this location.

NEWTOWNARDS   J492738

The Castle Garden Spinning Mills lie within a area 210m by 150m enclosed by a garden wall 3m high with circular flankers at the SW and SE corners. These are a relic of Newtown House built between 1608 and 1618 by Sir Hugh Montgomery incorporating the claustral buildings of a priory. It was gutted by fire in 1664 and replaced by a new house by Sir Robert Colville, who acquired the site in 1675. Only its gatehouse remained by 1744. Between it and the priory church are shapeless remains of what may be the "stump of an old castle in Newtown" occupied by Sir Hugh whilst his house was being built.

PORTAFERRY   J593508   C

Above the harbour is a 16th century tower built by the Savage family. It has an entrance onto the foot of a stair in a wing 4.5m wide projecting 3m from the SW side of a main block 10.3m by 9.8m. The stair rises only to the next storey, and a spiral stair in the west corner then leads to the third storey and wall-walk, which allows three levels of rooms to be accommodated in the upper parts of the wing. The upper parts of the main block now lack their eastern corner. Beside the wing is the chimney stack of a lost second storey fireplace in the SW wall.

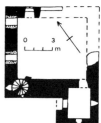

Portaferry Castle: plan

Quoile Castle

Portaferry Castle

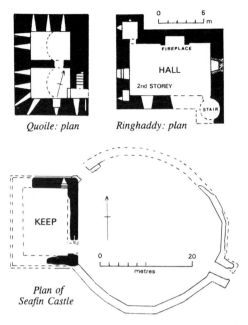

Quoile: plan   Ringhaddy: plan

Plan of
Seafin Castle

Ringhaddy Castle

QUINTIN   J632505

The Smith family had a tower here by the 1580s, when it is shown on Lord Burghley's map. It was sold to Sir James Montgomery, who remodelled the tower and added a bawn with flankers and an outbuilding containing a kitchen c1630. The ruinous tower was incorporated into a house and given new battlements in the mid 19th century. It measures 9m by 7.7m over walls 1.2m thick and originally had one storey over a vault and two below, but in the rebuilding just one room 7.5m high was created under the vault.

QUOILE   J496470   A

This ruined late 16th century tower measuring 10.8m by 8.1m was repaired in the 1980s and made safe following the collapse of one of the upper corners. It was occupied by the West family until at least the mid 18th century. The lowest level contains two vaulted cellars each furnished with five gunloops. From the entrance with a drawbar slot a straight stair in the east wall leads to the second storey, also now subdivided. A stair in the north wall then leads to the single room on the third storey, which had wooden lintelled windows. Both upper storeys have fireplaces.

RINGHADDY   J538588

Ringhaddy belonged to the Mandevilles from the 13th century until the 16th century, when it passed to the Whytes, from whom it went to the Hamiltons in the 17th century. It has both a motte and a castle in the form of a block 11.5m by 8.3m with square projecting turrets at diagonally opposite corners to contain the latrines and the now destroyed staircase. Traces remain of a former vault over the lowest storey which is 15th century work. The walls above are slightly thicker, suggesting rebuilding of the upper levels c1600. The hall has a fireplace and several altered windows. There were bedrooms above and then attics with gabled roofs rising direct from the outer walls although battlements with open wall-walks must have been intended originally.

Strangford Castle

Skettrick Castle

SEAFIN   J220388

Only footings remain of a wall surrounding a polygonal court 30m across on a hillock. A tower on the SE contained a postern but the main gateway lay on the NW beside a hall keep 19m long by 14.5m of which the east wall survives 2m high with part of a doorway with a drawbar slot and stubs of the south and north end walls. This castle was built by Justiciar Maurice Fitzgerald in 1252 but was captured and wrecked by Brian O'Neill the following year and not restored until after Brian's death at the Battle of Down in 1260. It was later probably occupied by the Magennis family. See pages 7 and 49.

SKETTRICK   J524625   A

The MacQuillans' tower by the causeway approach to Skettrick Island was seized by the Clannaboy O'Neills but returned by Henry O'Neill in 1470. Access to the island was by a 2.7m wide passageway through the base of a tower 15.4m by 9m with a narrow vaulted guardroom on one side and a cellar on the other later made into a kitchen and now lacking its vault. A mural stair in the east wall led to two upper storeys, now very ruined since the west wall facing the causeway and containing their latrines had fallen. In the 16th century the passageway was blocked up, a small bawn built around the northern end of the tower and the inner end of the guard room walled off to form a prison. A water supply was brought into the bawn from some distance away by means of a long tunnel.

STRANGFORD   J589498   E

A squat 16th century tower 7.5m square over walls 1m thick guards the port. There are three unvaulted storeys and there was probably also once an attic within the battlements, where there is a machicolation defending the entrance. There are no stone stairs and communication between the levels is by wooden steps and hatchways in the floors.

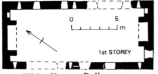

White House, Ballyspurge

Strangford: plan

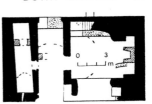

Plan of Skettrick Castle

WALSHESTOWN   J545498

This 16th century tower measuring 8.7m by 8m has four storeys all with altered windows, a low pitched roof and stepped battlements with square turrets rising above diagonally opposite corners. From the entrance in the NE end wall a straight stair leads up to the hall, another stair leads to the third storey and a spiral stair then rises to the third storey. Access to the wall-walk is by a trap door in the roof of a chamber in the north corner, below which is a latrine. The second storey has a blocked fireplace in the SW wall. This end of the tower is still enclosed by a loopholed bawn wall 2.5m high. See page 10.

WHITE HOUSE, BALLYSPURGE   J643551

Patrick Savage built this single storey house 16m long by 7m wide with fireplaces at each end in the 1640s. It lies in the east corner of a fragmentary bawn 30m by 22m with a gateway on the SW side, both the bawn wall and house having several gunloops.

OTHER CASTLE REMAINS IN COUNTY DOWN

CARLINGFORD LOUGH J253098 Fragmentary 16th century U-shaped blockhouse 13m
   by 7m with gunports in walls 0.9m thick commanding lough near Haulbowline light.
CASTLEBOY J625557 Latrine turret three storeys high projecting beyond base of east
   wall of tower 10m by 8m. A second turret on this side probably contained a staircase.
CASTLE ISLAND J516468 Lower part of west wall 1.5m thick of tower 7m wide with
   traces of three loops (including one facing north) on shore beside causeway.
CASTLE SKREEN J466400 6m high latrine turret 2.5m wide above refaced base is relic
   of a tower house located one side of a ringfort. See page 9.
RATHFRILAND J202337 Lower part of SE wall of tower 8m square. Traces of entrance
   with drawbar-slot and stair. Occupied by Hugh Magennis in the 1580s. Ruin by 1744.
WOODGRANGE J444465 A low fragment of the 1.3m thick wall of a tower with one
   loop lies on the edge of a ringfort.

CASTLE SITES IN COUNTY DOWN

ANNADORN J426452 Approximate site of the seat of the MacCartanes.
ARDKEEN J593571 Site of tower house built on motte
BONECASTLE J464415 Slight traces of walls below ground. History unknown.
LOUGHBRICKLAND J112414 Possible site of Sir Marmaduke Whitchurch's castle of
   1585 replacing a nearby Magennis castle destroyed by the Earl of Ormond in 1424.
NEWCASTLE J376310 Magennis castle by shore replaced c1830 by Annesley Arms
   Hotel. Dated 1588 over the entrance but may have existed as early as 1433.
RATHMULLAN J477374 Work on reservoir revealed part of base of tower 7.3m wide
   with 3.3m wide turret projecting 2m from west wall.
ROSEMOUNT J585678 House of c1740 on site of Sir James Montgomery's house of
   1634 burnt downt in 1695. A document of 1691 describes it as having two flankers.
ROSSTREVOR J170180 Stronghouse of 1611-12, possibly replacing a Magennis castle.
SAUL Harris in 1744 mentions a tower to SW of church having two turrets but no stair.
OTHER CASTLE SITES: Annacloy J450480, Castle Dorras J486447, Castle Espie
J486673, Inishargy J605647, Kilbride J540350, Lismolyn J560424, Loughadian
J060394, Moira J149609, Rathgorman J527582, Ringdufferin J537567, Scarva J065437.

GAZETTEER OF CASTLES IN COUNTY FERMANAGH

AGHALINE   H341200   D

On a hillock near the border with County Cavan are overgrown remains of a wall 3m high around a bawn 19m wide built by Thomas Crichton c1615-8, and abandoned c1700 when the family moved to Crom. On the southern corners are circular flankers 5m in diameter with gunloops in the form of slits, diamond-shaped loops and crossloops.

CASTLE ARCHDALE   H187599   A

In the wooded demesne of the house of 1773 are fragments of a stronghouse 21.4m long built by John Archdale in 1615, wrecked by Rory Maguire in 1641 and burnt in 1689. The house had two storeys and attic rooms in the roof. It had a wooden staircase in a wing with gunloops set in the middle of the north side, where the ground sloped away. On the other side was a bawn 19m square with a Latin inscription dated 1615 over its gateway in the south wall, recently rebuilt to stand without the buttresses later provided. There are no remains of the square flankers that originally lay at either end of this side.

CASTLE BALFOUR   H362337   E

Sir James Balfour's stronghouse of 1618 has a wing on a low cliff on the west and originally there was a bawn 21m square on the flat eastern side. Over a vaulted kitchen with a large fireplace in the wing and two small cellars in the adjoining part of the main block lay a hall reached by a wide scale-and-platt staircase in the northern part of the main block. The entrance lies in a projecting bay at the foot of this stair, which has lost its steps. The main block continues to the south and has a spiral stair in a turret corbelled out in the angle between it and another wing to the east. At the summit are parapets upon rows of small square corbels. The castle was refortified by General Ludlow in 1652. It was burnt in 1689 but restored and inhabited until c1820. See page 9 and 52.

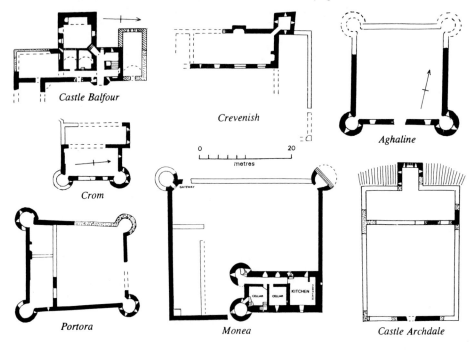

Castle Balfour

Crevenish

Aghaline

Crom

0   20
metres

Portora

Monea

Castle Archdale

Crevenish Castle

Castle Archdale

CASTLE CALDWELL   H017605   C

Much of the present heavily overgrown ruin dates from the 1790s but the west front has a pair of three storey 17th century flankers bristling with vertical slit gunloops. The house was originally called Rossbeg and was built by Sir Francis Blennerhasset in 1612. It was renamed after being sold in 1671 to Sir James Caldwell, an Enniskillen merchant created a baronet in 1683. In the early 19th century it passed on the death of the 6th baronet to the Bloomfields, who were in residence until are fire c1905.

CORRATRASNA   H274300   D

The ruined gables and footings of the side walls remain of a two storey stronghouse probably built by the Balfours c1610. It measures 13m by 7m and has fireplaces at each level and gunloops on the upper storey. To the south are traces of an earth rampart or terrace. See page 56.

CREVENISH   H165626

At the NW corner of Thomas Blennerhasset's three storey stronghouse of c1615 is a tower about 4.6m square with gunloops and an acute outermost angle. There are slight remains of a second tower embedded in farm buildings to the NE and it is likely that there were once a full set of four, those by the house being of four storeys and those on the bawn wall having two or three storeys. The house was 8.4m wide over walls 1m thick. The only features are some brick fireplaces and large crude east windows with timber lintels over the embrasures. In 1641 Crevenish was the home of Lady Deborah Blennerhasset and her second husband Captain Rory Maguire who destroyed many of his Protestant neighbours' houses during the Catholic revolt of that year. Sir William Cole and other local lords were warned of the danger whilst dining at the castle and made their escape. Part of the castle was later used as a church and its bawn about 22m square became a cemetery.

Moulded corbelling at Enniskillen

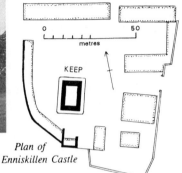

Crom Castle

Plan of Enniskillen Castle

CROM   H364238   E

According to the surveyor Captain Pynnar the bawn of Michael Balfour's house begun in 1611 was 18m square with a wall 3.6m high. It was sold to Sir Stephen Butler in 1619, and to Abraham Crichton of Aghalane c1660, and withstood two attacks by Jacobites in 1689. The house accidentally caught fire in 1764 whilst the Crichtons were away at a party at Florence Court. By Upper Lough Erne are remains of a house 13.6m long by 7.8m wide with round flankers 4.5m in diameter on the eastern corners. The NE flanker stands three storeys high with two vaults, and there is also a high fragment of the north end of a square NW wing. The wing walls extending to thinly-walled towers to the east and west are later ornamental ruins but the lower part of the round tower with 1.2m thick walls with a battered base by the lough shore may be a relic of the bawn. See page 52.

ENNISKILLEN   H231442   E

A drawing made by a soldier during the siege of 1595 when Captain John Dowdall captured the castle shows a bawn beside the River Erne with a large embattled four storey tower on the east side and a smaller tower beside the gateway on the north. All that remains from that period is the massively walled lowest part of the tower house with a crossloop at the south end. It is thought to have been built c1415-20 by Hugh Maguire "The Hospitable" but it is first mentioned in 1439 when the Maguire chief was taken prisoner there. The Maguires recaptured the castle not long after the siege of 1595 and lost it once more before the water-borne attack of 1602 led by Niall Garbh O'Donnell, during which it was wrecked. In 1607 Enniskillen was granted to Captain William Cole, who built a stronghouse upon the stump of the old tower house and rebuilt the bawn wall to a height of 7.8m with a wall-walk and four flankers, two circular and two angular. The family lived alongside the castle in a timber-framed house. In c1615-20 he added the Watergate, a rectangular three storey tower containing a well and having a lofty pair of conical-roofed round bartizans corbelled out from the corners projecting beyond the bawn wall, although there is no sign of an actual gateway. Cole was knighted in 1618 and managed to hold out against Rory Maguire in 1641. The castle also held out against James II's Lord Lieutenant Tyrconnell in 1690. The castle was refurbished as a barracks from 1796, the main block being mostly rebuilt and much of the bawn wall removed.

MONEA H165494 A

Malcolm Hamilton, Rector of Devenish and Chancellor of Down erected this stronghouse c1615-18, the bawn being added just prior to his elevation to the see of Cashel in 1623. It was captured during the 1641 rising, but the castle survived unharmed during the war of 1689-91, when it was the home of Gustavus Hamilton, Governor of Enniskillen, and it remained occupied until an accidental fire in the mid 18th century. The building reflects the Scottish origin of the builder. Lying on the south side of a bawn 32m by 28m with remains of circular flankers on the northern corners and footing of a bawn on the west side is a mansion 17.4m long by 8.9m wide with a pair of circular towers 5m in diameter on the western corners. A gunloop in one covers the entrance onto the foot of the staircase in the other. This connected with a passage leading past separate cellars for food and wine to a kitchen at the east end. The wine cellar and kitchen each have service stairs up to the hall, east of which was a drawing room placed over the warmth of the kitchen. The third storey contained three main bedrooms, two of which were reached by a continuation of the service stair up from the kitchen. Only one of the two conical-roofed round bartizans at the east end now survives. The roof was thatched, contrary to the usual Scottish practice of slate or tile roofing. At this level there are diagonally-set square caphouses over the western towers. See pages 9, 52 and 56.

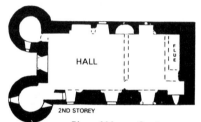

Plan of Monea Castle

Water Gate at Enniskillen

Interior of Monea Castle

Monea Castle

Monea Castle

Interior of Tully Castle

Corratrasna

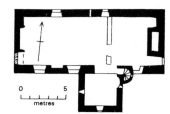

Plan of Tully Castle

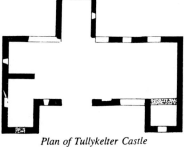

Portora Castle

Plan of Tullykelter Castle

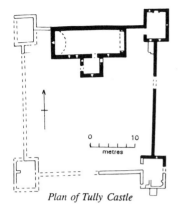

Plan of Tully Castle

Tully Castle

PORTORA   H222453   A

Despite damage to it caused by an explosion made by the boys of Portora School in 1859, and the gales of 1894, three-quarters of Sir William Cole's bawn of c1615 remains complete. It measures 21.5m by 18m inside a wall 0.9m thick with four circular flankers 4.8m in diameter furnished with gunloops. Little remains of the NE flanker and not much survives of the low house 6.8m wide occupying the western third of the bawn apart from a large fireplace, probably part of the kitchen. The Coles lived here until they transferred to Florence Court in 1764. See page 52.

TULLY   H127566   E

The house and bawn built c1615-8 by Sir John Hume from Manderston in Berwickshire has been a ruin since Christmas Day 1641 when Captain Rory Maguire captured and burnt it, most of the occupants being slaughtered. The bawn 30m square had a wall 0.7m thick with a gateway on the south side and four corner flankers each 7m long by 5.5m wide. Most of the eastern parts survive but very little remains of the western wall and its flankers. The house lies on the north, the higher part of the site, overlooking Lough Erne. It is 16.6m long by 6.8m wide and has a vaulted basement with a kitchen fireplace with shelving at the east end. A wing on the south side contained a timber stair from an entrance with a drawbar slot up to a hall and chamber over the vault. There were bedrooms within the roof reached by a narrow stair in a corbelled-out turret.

OTHER CASTLE REMAINS IN COUNTY FERMANAGH

DRUMBROUGHA'S H394245 Long section of featureless walling by shore of Upper
    Lough Erne.
TULLYKELTER H155483 James Summerville's house of c1620 is a thinly-walled
    structure with three wings but no surviving defensive features.
A house lies on the site of Brian Maguire's house at Tullyweel H412480.
A 16th century sketch shows a tall tower within an unflanked bawn at BELLEEK.
CASTLE SITES: Aghagay H416261, Aghalun H387410, Agharoosky H449282,
    Agheeghter H450463, Belleisle H289355, Callowhill H277264, Cornagrade H232449,
    Corrard H300346, Fargrim H444272, Horse Island H197536, Inishcreenry H305334,
    Inishfendra H380232, Inishleague H299327, Magherameenagh G978592, Manor Water
    House H374311, Naan Island H294318, Necarne H236573, Rathmoran H436310,
    Rossclare H192543, Tharlegh H315428

GAZETTEER OF CASTLES IN COUNTY LONDONDERRY

BALLYKELLY C624226

The Fishmongers' Company built a 3.6m high wall here c1615 around a bawn enclosing the house of their agent Mr Higgins which was later leased to the Hamiltons and then Beresfords. The latter c1730 replaced a corner flanker with a new house named Walworth. The other flankers still survive, one being a polygonal salient bastion and the other two circular towers of two storeys. The Fishmongers regained possession in 1820.

BALLYREAGH C846399

In the late 1960s the local authority removed a 17m length of walling 1.2m thick and 4m high containing musket loops and set on the inner edge of a ditch isolating a promontory rising 15m above the sea. The castle belonged to the McHenrys, who fled when Lord Deputy Sir John Perrot approached the site with heavy artillery in 1584.

BELLAGHY H953963 E

A report of 1622 describes the Vintners' Company as having here a house with two round towers of brick with domed roofs. One is still represented by the structure adjoining the existing house, built after the MacDonnells burnt the 30m wide bawn during the rebellion of 1641 and now a visitors' centre. The other tower has been revealed by excavations which also showed that the leaning section of bawn wall (now shored up) was built over the ditch of a ringfort. The side of the bawn containing the gateway has been destroyed but two rectangular flankers of differing sizes still remain.

BRACKFIELD C511097 A

The 18.6m square bawn built by the Skinners' Company c1615 is well preserved although the gateway has been widened and only the outer wall with two fireplace recesses remains of the house. The wall is 0.8m thick, 3m high and has 3.6m high bastions 4.5m in diameter set at diagonally opposite corners, one of which has partly fallen.

King's House bawn at Dungiven

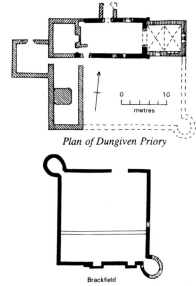

Plan of Dungiven Priory

0   10
metres

Brackfield

Old sketch of Brackfield Bawn

Brackfield Bawn

COLERAINE   C844325

Nothing remains of Thomas MacUchtry's castle of 1214, probably a wooden structure on a motte. Coleraine was protected by the River Bann on the west and work began in 1610 under Sir Thomas Phillips on enclosing the other sides with earth ramparts with angled-bastions fronted by a ditch up to 12m wide and 1m deep, the work being mostly completed by November 1612. Later proposals for stone defences, and in particular the replacement of the timber-framed gatehouses, came to nothing. The town withstood an attack by the Irish in 1641 and was taken by General Monck in 1648. A new Cromwellian fort begun in the 1650s was never completed. Nothing remains of it but part of the base remains of the northern section of the town rampart, which was remarkably thin (about 3m) for such an earthwork.

CULMORE   C477223

An early 19th century folly stands on the site of an earthwork fort established by Sir Henry Docwra in May 1600 around an older tower 6.3m square. The fort had been rebuilt in stone by 1618 and a report of 1622 mentions it as being triangular with pairs of demi-bastions on the corners of the 30m long landward wall, which was 4.2m high. There were twelve guns mounted "en barbette", and the commander lived in a house of two storeys and an attic adjoining the old tower. New outer fortifications begun in the 1650s were demolished following Major Legge's report of 1662 about them.

DUNGIVEN   C692091 & C692082 A

Nothing remains of the principal castle of the O'Kanes or O'Cahans at Dungiven. The King's House, a bawn 60m by 48m built by James I, was later granted to the Skinners' Company. Of it there remain half of the 0.8m thick and 4m high east wall with a modern gateway, and part of the west wall and a square NW flanker. Upper firing embrasures were served by a platform on arches, the last remains of which were removed in 1972. A house of 1832 lies on the south side.

   In 1982 excavations at the ruins of the Augustinian priory to the south revealed footings of a second house and bawn built there by Sir Edward Doddington before 1611. The 12th century nave and the 13th century vaulted chancel remained in use as such for another century. The later medieval tower became part of a house with a range of two storeys and an attic added south of it. The wide base in the middle of the range supported a chimneybreast. A scullery wing was added on the west to mask the junction of the two parts, whilst the former cloister became a bawn with a small SE corner flanker and an outbuilding on the south side. Sir Edward's widow lived here until the house was captured by the Irish in 1641. It was re-occupied later but then burnt down accidentally.

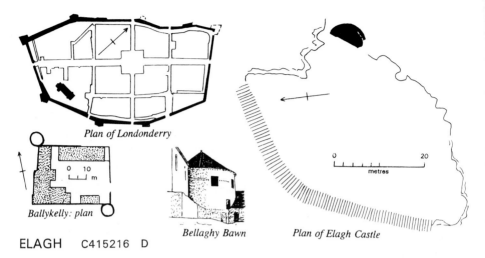

Plan of Londonderry

Ballykelly: plan

Bellaghy Bawn

Plan of Elagh Castle

ELAGH   C415216   D

Near the east corner of a platform about 23m across on outcrop of schist by a farm is a 7.5m high fragment of a solid D-shaped tower 6.5m in diameter with evidence of a gateway on its east side, where the rock has been quarried away. On the west side the structure shows evidence of two periods of work, the round face being a later addition. This O'Doherty seat was captured in May 1600 by Sir Henry Docwra and then garrisoned with 150 men.

LONDONDERRY   C435168   E

Derry was given earthwork defences in 1566 by Colonel Edward Randolph but it was abandoned after the magazine in the cathedral exploded and wrecked the whole town. It was refortified with new earth ramparts after being recovered for Elizabeth I by Sir Henry Docwra in 1600 but was captured in 1608 by Sir Cahir O'Doherty. After James I granted Derry and an enormous surrounding estate to the City of London in 1613 (hence the official name Londonderry) work was begun under Peter Benson to a design by Captain Edward Doddington on a 7m high stone outer face rising with a slope up to a string-course, above which are artillery embrasures. The rampart has an earth core and varies from 4m to 9m wide. Now the most complete system of their type and period remaining in the British Isles, these defences enclose an area 450m long by 260m wide. From the central square or diamond four main roads lead to the Shipquay Gate facing NE, the Butcher Gate facing NW, the Bishop Gate facing SW and the Ferryquay Gate facing SE, all the gates having been rebuilt during the 18th and 19th centuries. There were also three other minor gateways, probably all later insertions. One of these is named Castle Gate in memory of the vanished O'Doherty castle which guarded the lowest crossing of the River Foyle. The rectangular Hangman's Bastion on the NW side and five angular bastions survive intact, but not much remains of the Gunner's Bastion north of the Butcher Gate, or of the Coward's Bastion (demolished in 1824) and Water Bastion at either end of the NE side. On and near the Church Bastion near the cathedral in the southern corner are two circular sentinel turrets added in 1627. There was a ditch around the SE and SW sides of the city and a natural slope beyond the other sides. The walls withstood attacks by the Confederate Irish in 1641, and a Parliamentary garrison under Sir Charles Coote held out against Royalists in 1648-9. During the winter of 1688-9 the city withstood attacks by James II's forces for 105 days until a relief force arrived by sea and broke the boom or barrier extending across the mouth of the river. Although much damage was done by James' artillery he lacked sufficiently heavy guns to force a breach in the ramparts.

Sentry Box upon Londonderry town walls

Elagh Castle

MONEYMORE   H858833

Behind the Orange Hall are slight traces of the Drapers' Company's 30m square bawn which was replaced by a public house c1760. One of the two diagonally opposite corner flankers adjoined the three bay house of three storeys and an attic. The wall (according to Pynnar) was 4.5m high. Phillip's survey of 1622 shows the bawn as having a timber-framed gatehouse, and notes the house as having been left incomplete without floors or roof, the tenant Sir Thomas Roper being an absentee. Cormick O'Hagan sacked the town in 1641 and held the castle for the Confederate Irish for several years.

Londonderry town walls

Londonderry town walls

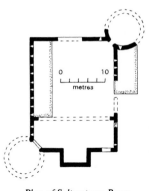

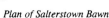

Plan of Salterstown Bawn

Salterstown Bawn

SALTERSTOWN   H951824   D

Very little survives of the large (8m diameter) flankers set at the NW and SE corners of a bawn measuring 23m by 19m built by the Salters' Company of London c1615 to guard a port on Lough Neagh, and the bawn wall remains are incorporated into farm buildings. Lofty fragments remain of the south gable of the house in the western part of the bawn and the wing later added to the middle of the west side to contain a scale-and-platt staircase. The bawn was captured by the Confederate Irish in 1641.

OTHER CASTLE REMAINS IN COUNTY LONDONDERRY

AGIVEY C902226 Remains of cellars below present house. House had four turrets. Bawn
    unflanked and shown in 1622 survey as partly of wood. Burnt by rebel Irish in 1642.
MAGHERAFELT H897906 Stronghouse and bawn with two square flankers and one
    spear-head shaped flanker stood near the Diamond. Burnt by the Irish in 1641 and by
    the Jacobites in 1689.

CASTLE SITES IN COUNTY LONDONDERRY

AGHADOWNEY C858209 Farm buildings on site. House demolished in 1970s had old
    parts.
ANAGH C473193 Site of tower set on crannog.
ARDMORE C677204 Former O'Kane tower said to have measured 9m by 6m
BALLYNEILL H928853 Site of house and bawn of the Nieves family.
CLONDERMOT Goldsmiths' Company bawn SE of Derry shown on 1622 survey as having
    three corner flankers, one with conical roof. Round end bay of house at fourth corner.
LIMAVADY C677204 Site of O'Kane castle remodelled c1610-20 by Sir Thomas Phillips.
    It withstood an Irish attack in 1641 but was captured and destroyed in 1642.
LOUGHAN ISLAND C877288 Site of castle captured by O'Donnells in 1544.
MOVANAGHER C920159 End wall of house with conical-roofed corner flankers adjoined
    wall of bawn also with three conical-roofed flankers. Built by Mercers' Company.
MUFF C529203 Site of house and bawn besieged by the Irish in 1641.
REDCASTLE C847308 Site of castle of the George family.
OTHER CASTLE SITES: Annaghmore H929913, Ballindreen C901306, Ballycastle
    C677270, Castledawson H928934, Castleroe C860230, Craig C713339, Dromore
    876289, Duncruin C685325, Killane C681239, Lewis C511147, Macosquin C825288,
    Primity C412127, Rowleys H829960

GAZETTEER OF CASTLES IN COUNTY MONAGHAN

DRUMMOND   H841035

Thomas Raven's drawing of 1634 depicts the house and bawn then recently built by Robert Devereux, 3rd Earl of Essex, which was destroyed in the wars of 1689-91, leaving no traces. The house had three wings on one side facing towards where the bawn had a show front with a central gatehouse and two storey circular corner flankers with pyramidal roofs. There were service ranges along two sides of the bawn but the far wall was without either buildings or flankers, although it had a back gateway.

MAGHERNACLOY   N853975

The Hadsells' 17th century house has one full storey over vaulted cellars and double-stepped battlements surrounding attic rooms in the roof. There is a wing on the north side and another at the SE corner. The south doorway and sash windows are later insertions.

MANNAN   H853074   A

Dating probably from the 1240s are fragments of stonework upon Peter Pipard's impressive motte of 1193 and inner bailey 40m long by up to 28m wide. Both parts are surrounded by a ditch but an outer bailey 40m wide extending 70m further SE has just a scarp. A stone causeway connects the inner bailey and the motte summit, which bears evidence of a building about 16m by 10m with a court 15m across SE of it.

OTHER CASTLE REMAINS IN COUNTY MONAGHAN

CLONBOY H496253 Ditched platform 19m square of uncertain date.
CROSSMOYLE H500258 Ditched motte with rectangular bailey built and destroyed in
    1212. Traces of possible bawn flankers of the 1630s in bailey north and west corners.
INISHKEEN H932067 High walled bawn with archway and footings of internal gatehouse
    to NE of bailey beside large motte.
MAGHERNACLOY N853975 Remains of the Hadsells' late 16th century stronghouse.
ROOSKY H673337 Oval natural spur with traces of ditch on NW side.

CASTLE SITES IN COUNTY MONAGHAN

CASTLE BLAYNEY Sir Edward Blayney's bawn of c1610 about 60m square had 5.5m
    high wall with four flankers, two round and two square. H-shaped house inside.
FEAHOE N852956 Supposed site of castle destroyed during 17th century.
GLASLOUGH Unlocated site of 50m square bawn built by Sir Thomas Ridgway.
MONAGHAN H672337 Last remains of Sir Edward Blaney's tower and bawn of c1611
    vanished c1853. No remains of nearby star fort of c1602 or town ditch and gates.
Possible McMahon castles: Conaghy, Conra, Dawsongrove, Killcoonagh and Killykeseame.
McCrea's map of 1793 shows castles at Ballyleck and Derrynashallog.

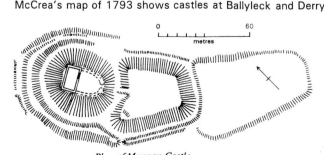

Plan of Mannan Castle

Stronghouse at Maghernacloy

GAZETTEER OF CASTLES IN COUNTY TYRONE

AUGHENTAINE   H498515   D

Sir William Stewart's stronghouse of c1620 was probably never restored after being burnt by Sir Phelim O'Neill in 1641, but it remained almost intact until the south wall collapsed in 1935. It had a wing 6.8m wide in the middle of the north wall of a block 6.6m wide and about 16m long. The surviving west gable has fireplaces serving the second and third storeys and the attic rooms in the roof. Access from the hall and drawing room on the second storey to the bedrooms above was by a spiral stair in a turret supported upon moulded corbelling over the NW re-entrant angle.

AUGHER or SPUR ROYAL   H561538   D

At the Plantation of Ulster much of the barony of Clogher went to the Ridgeway brothers. George had 1,000 acres and in 1611 began a bawn which has not survived, whilst Sir Thomas, with a lucrative treasury office, ended up with 4,300 acres. He built the house at Augher but in 1622 sold his Irish estates to Sir James Erskine in return for a grant of the earldom of Londonderry. The alternative name Spur Royal refers to the remarkable plan of the stronghouse at Augher, a square of 9m with a triangular bay in the middle of each side, creating an eight-pointed shape like a rowel or spiked wheel on a riding spur. The tower has three storeys and battlements with the merlons sloped on the outside face. A machicolation decorated with a spiral wheel protects the entrance doorway on the east. The basement windows are 19th century but the labelled mouldings and chamfered frames of the upper windows are original. Just one circular flanker remains of the bawn. Although the main tower looks like a Jacobean folly it was strong enough to hold out against Sir Phelim O'Neill in 1641, but it was burnt by the Jacobites in 1689. It was not restored until 1827-32, when a long house was added by Sir James Bunbury on one side.

BELTRIM   H489864

Alterations and extensions in the 18th and 19th centuries have obliterated most of William Hamilton's house of c1610 above the Owenkillew River, but the garden wall to the east incorporates part of the bawn including the shell of a circular flanker and a round tower of rubble, as well as a more picturesque turret with windows dated 1785.

Aughentaine Castle

Augher or Spur Royal

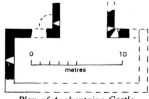

Plan of Aughentaine Castle

BENBURB H815520 D

Sean "The Proud" O'Neill's chief house at Benburb was burnt by the English in 1566 but was repaired and used by Turlough O'Neill until 1573. Its ruins were subsequently plundered for materials to build the fort at Blackwatertown. After being granted 1,000 acres here in 1611 Sir Richard Wingfield built a bawn 39m by 33m upon a cliff 36m above the Blackwater River. It is enclosed by a loopholed wall 4.8m high with a coped top. There is a circular stair turret at the SW corner and the NW and NE corners have square towers containing rooms lighted by mullion-and-transom windows, whilst the gateway lies between them. A later house in the SE corner has replaced another flanker. The bawn was sacked by the O'Neills in 1641 and was dismantled by Owen Roe O'Neill soon after his victory here over the Ulster Scots led by General Munro.

CASTLE CAULFIELD H755626 A

Of the O'Donnellys' 16th century bawn there remains the gatehouse, a building 12.3m by 6.9m with guard rooms on either side of a central passage, the western room having a fireplace and the well of a stair to the lost upper storey in a projecting turret. The passage has three murder holes in the vault but the rebates of the gates have gone. Adjoining the gatehouse is the NW wing of Sir Toby Caulfield's three storey mansion of begun c1611 and described in 1619 by Pynnar as the "fairest building in- the North". Sir Toby administered the O'Neill lands in Tyrone after the flight of Earl Hugh to Spain in 1607. The dispossessed O'Donnellys burnt the house in 1641 but the Caulfiends, later made Viscounts Charlement, restored it in the 1660s. In 1670 the first Viscount allowed the Catholic primate Oliver Plunkett to use the courtyard for ordinations. John Wesley preached at the gate in 1767, although by then the house was abandoned. It has a main block 25.4m long by 8.6m wide with a pair of chimney breasts on the east side capped by octagonal chimneys. Little remains of the SW wing but the NW wing also has a projecting chimney breast. Sandstone stringcourses mark the floor levels but most of the large mullion-and-transom windows have been torn out and their embrasures blocked up.

Old view of Benburb Castle

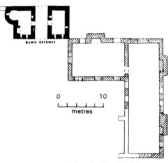

Plan of Castle Caulfield

Castle Caulfield

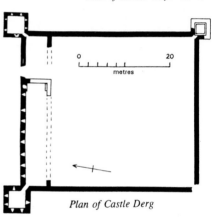

Castle Curlews: gunloop

Plan of Favour Royal Bawn

Castle Derg

CASTLE CURLEWS   H320758   D

The surviving fragment of the stronghouse built by Sir John Davies before 1619 has a room 6.4m square with fireplaces in the NE wall and in the west and south corners and evidence of large bay windows facing NW, SW, and SE. The lower part of the SE bay survives with two gunloops opening out of a low basement room below. The house seems to have continued to the NE and had a bawn about 25m by 33m to the NW.

Plan of Castle Derg

CASTLEDERG   H 260844   A

Sir John Davies, Irish Attorney General and Speaker in the Irish House of Commons built a bawn above the north bank of the River Derg c1615. It passed via his daughter Lucy to the Earls of Huntingdon and withstood an attack by Sir Phelim O'Neill in 1641 but the damage then done to it was never repaired. The bawn measures 34m by 30m and retains most of its loopholed north wall with a square flanker at either end. It was entered through a house of which only the east gable and a brick-lined oven in the middle now remain. The bawn encloses the site of an O'Donnell tower house captured in 1497 by Henry O'Neill and recaptured by the O'Donnells in 1505 and again in 1508.

CASTLE MERVYN   H335576

One end gable three storeys high with a chimney stack for a fireplace with an oven at ground level is all that remains of Lord Castlehaven's house of c1630 also known as Trillick. It measured 14m long by 6.5m wide.

DERRYWOONE   H367835

Near the late 18th century house of the Hamilton Earls of Abercorn in the Baronscourt demesne is a ruined L-plan house of c1625 with a circular flanking tower 5m across on the outermost corner. The re-entrant angle has a stair turret on moulded corbelling giving access from the hall and drawing room on the second storey to the bedrooms above and the attic rooms in the roof. The main block 7.7m wide contained a kitchen at ground level. It now ends to the west with an inserted crosswall. The building has large upper windows and lacks any defensive features.

Castle Curlews

Castle Mervyn

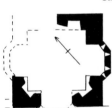

Castle Curlews: plan

Castle Mervyn: plan

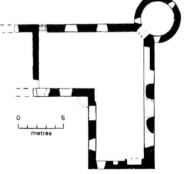

Plan of Derrywoone Castle

DUNGANNON H799626

Dungannon was the chief seat of the O'Neills, who were created Earls of Tyrone after Con O'Neill submitted to Henry VIII in 1542. Their castle here was captured in 1498 by the 8th Earl of Kildare, then Lord Deputy, and was destroyed by the O'Donnells in 1590. After Hugh O'Neill fled to Spain in 1607 Dungannon went to Sir Arthur Chichester who replaced what remained of the castle with a bawn 36m square with a deep stone-lined ditch and four square corner flankers. It was taken by Sir Phelim O'Neill in 1641 and destroyed in 1646. The round tower on the site is a relic of a mansion built here c1790 by Thomas Knox Harrington.

FAVOUR ROYAL H631538

A bawn begun by George Ridgeway in 1611 passed to his brother Thomas and was later transferred to Sir James Erskine. The name Favour Royal commemorates Charles I's charter of 1630 ratifying the agreement. The bawn was abandoned in 1670 when one of Sir James' granddaughters, then married to John Moutray, moved into a new house to the SW. Defaced walls 0.9m thick enclose a court 24m square with a circular flanker 4.2m in diameter at each corner. Little remains of the northern flankers and the wall between the east gateway and the NE flanker has gone entirely.

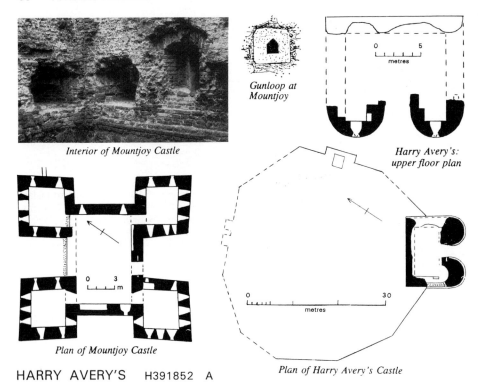

Interior of Mountjoy Castle

Gunloop at Mountjoy

Harry Avery's: upper floor plan

Plan of Mountjoy Castle

Plan of Harry Avery's Castle

HARRY AVERY'S   H391852   A

The name is a corruption of that of the likely builder, Henry Aimbredh O'Neill, who died in 1392. His castle was destroyed by the English in 1609 and plundered for materials to build the castle and town of Newtownstewart. On a hilltop are footings of a curtain wall around a polygonal bailey 32m across with a square tower on the east side and what at first looks like a gatehouse on the south. This building has a pair of 6m diameter towers with solid bases flanking an entrance in the south wall of a main block 15m long by 9.4m wide over walls 2m thick. The entrance has lost its arch but retains a drawbar slot. It did not lead through into the court and the only further access was by a narrow stair in the west wall up to a hall which has been destroyed, although the towers survive to this level rooms with windows looking south. This rather unusual type of tower house may have originally had a third storey above.

KINARD   H754453

The 18th century Caludon House lies on the site of the O'Neill castle of Kinard replaced by a new house and bawn built c1619 by Turlough O'Neill, and itself destroyed by the O'Neills after their victory at Benburb in 1646. Cromwell later granted the estate to the Hamiltons.

MACHUGH   H364838

A crannog in Lough Catherine in the Baronscourt demesne (see also Derrywoone, p66) bears a 6m high tower measuring just 4.5m by 3.5m within walls 0.9m thick, the only features being the doorway and an east-facing window embrasure with a stepped square-corbelled roof. There are traces of a tiny bawn to the south and east.

MOUNTJOY   H901687   A

This building was completed in 1602 and named after Elizabeth I's viceroy Lord Mountjoy. Although planned like a private stronghouse with flankers 6.5m across at all four corners of a main block 11.8m by 8.2m it was a purely military outpost. The lower storey is faced with brick internally and the upper storey is faced with brick both inside and out. It was captured by Sir Phelim O'Neill in 1641 and burnt in 1642. It was soon re-occupied by the English but they in turn abandoned and burnt the fort to prevent the O'Neills occupying it. The fort was granted to the Earl of Dartmouth in 1683 and remained garrisoned during William III's reign. The outer defences shown on a survey of 1682 have gone.

NEWTOWNSTEWART   H402858   C

The south and west walls remain of Sir Robert Newcomen's three storey stronghouse which was about to be roofed at the time of Pynnar's survey of 1619. Then called Lislas, it was renamed after Sir William Stewart, who married Sir Robert's heiress c1628 and founded the present town. Both were burnt during James II's retreat from the siege of Derry in 1690. The house west wall has a circular stair turret whilst the south wall has windows of two and three lights with label mouldings and three gables with the central one surmounted by a brick chimney stack shaped in section like an eight-pointed stair.

OMAGH   H454727

Omagh is named after an O'Neill castle mentioned in 1470, the Oigh Maigh or seat of the chief, part of which seems to have survived until the 18th century. A fort with two full bastions and two demi-bastions and a timber-framed house built by Captain Ormon Leigh were destroyed in 1743 by a fire that consumed most of the town.

Harry Avery's Castle

Bawn gateway at Castle Caulfield

Mountjoy Castle

Newtownstewart Castle

Roughan Castle

ROUGHAN   H823683   A

Sir Andrew Stewart's stronghouse of 1618 was burnt by Sir Phelim O'Neill, who was captured on a nearby crannog in 1653 by William Caulfield and taken off to Dublin to be hanged. Now lying on the lawn of a later house used as retirement home, the house is a square of 8m over walls 1m thick and has corner towers containing rooms 2.5m in diameter. There are several gunloops in the lowest storey, where the only vaulting is that over a strongroom in the west tower, adjoining which is the scar of a destroyed bawn wall. The entrance lies in a rather indefensible position on the outer face of the north tower, which contained a spiral staircase. There are two upper storeys, both with fireplaces in the south-west wall, and there was an attic within the roof. The upper rooms in the east and west towers are square and also have fireplaces. Moulded string-courses mark the top and bottom of the topmost storey and a corbelled round arch links the west and south towers to provide a wall-walk behind the gable and chimney stack.

STRABANE   H347975

The town grew up around the vanished castle built by Earl of Abercorn in 1608. The Countess of Hamilton was captured when the castle fell to Sir Phelim O'Neill in 1641, but it was later recaptured by Colonel Hamilton. The town surrendered to James II in 1688 and was used as a base for the attack on Derry.

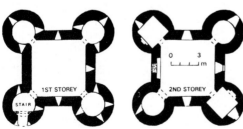

Plans of Roughan Castle

Roughan Castle

OTHER CASTLE REMAINS IN COUNTY TYRONE

BALLYGAWLEY H632575 Two towers remain on south side of bawn begun by William Turvey but sold in 1613.
MOUNTCASTLE C417051 6m high corner fragment of Sir Claud Hamilton's three storey house of 1619 with circular bartizan.

CASTLE SITES IN COUNTY TYRONE

BALLYMENAGH H821791 Last fragment levelled in the 1930s.
CLOGHFIN H574678 Former fragment of bawn south wall.
DUNNAMANAGH C446034 18th century gothick ruin by River Faughan on site of Sir John Drummond's bawn of c1610-19.
KNOCKMACLOY Granted to Turlough O'Neill in 1610.
MOYLE H411862 Platform 24m by 18m marked site of bawn.

Newtownstewart Castle

STEWARTSTOWN H860708 Named after Sir Andrew Stewart, whose bawn and house of 1608 are represented only by a platform measuring 60m by 35m.
OTHER CASTLE SITES: Castle Gore H253833, Castletown H706563, Roxborough H853566, The Bawn H713710

A GLOSSARY OF TERMS

Benburb: plan

ASHLAR - Masonry of blocks with even faces and square edges. BAILEY - Defensible space enclosed by a wall or a palisade and ditch. BARTIZAN - A turret corbelled out from the top of a corner. BASTION - Flanking projection of the same height as the main wall. BAWN - A court, usually stone walled. CAPHOUSE - Small square gabled space over a staircase or round projection. CASEMATE - A small vaulted chamber providing flanking fire along a wall. CORBEL - A projecting bracket supporting other stonework or timber beams. CRANNOG - A small artificial island occupied as a dwelling. HALL-HOUSE - A two storey building containing a hall or chamber over a basement. HARLING or ROUGHCAST - External coating of plaster with gravel and other coarse aggregate. HOODMOULD - Projecting moulding above an arch or lintel to throw off water. JAMB - the side of a doorway, window or other opening. KEEP - A citadel or ultimate strongpoint. The term is not medieval and such buildings were then called donjons. LIGHT - A compartment of a window. LOGGIA - Sheltered space behind a colonade. LOOP - A small opening for light or for the discharge of missiles. MACHICOLATION - A slot for dropping stones or shooting missiles at assailants. MOAT - a ditch, water-filled or dry, around an enclosure. MERLONS - The upstanding portions of a parapet, the cut-away parts between them being crenels. MOTTE - A steeply sided flat-topped mound, usually man-made. MULLION - A vertical member dividing the lights of a window. MURDER-HOLE - An internal machicolation, often in the vault of an entrance lobby. OGIVAL-ARCH - Arch of oriental origin with both convex and concave curves. PARAPET -A wall for protection at any sudden drop. PILASTER - A flat buttress. Commonly found on 12th and 13th century buildings. PLINTH - The projecting base of a wall. Usually battered (sloped) in Ireland rather than stepped. PORTCULLIS - Wooden gate designed to rise and fall in vertical grooves, being hoisted up with a windlass. POSTERN - A secondary gateway or doorway. A back entrance. QUOIN - Dressed (i.e. carefully shaped) stone at a corner of a building. SCALE-AND-PLATT STAIRCASE - Staircase with short straight flights and turns at landings. SOUTERRAIN - Underground stone-lined passage and chamber. A hiding place. SPANDREL - A surface between an arch and the rectangle containing it. STRONGHOUSE - A mansion capable of being defended against an attack. TOWER HOUSE - Self-contained house with the main rooms stacked vertically. TRACERY -Intersecting ribwork in the upper part of a later Gothic window. TRANSOM - A horizontal member dividing the lights of a window. WALL-WALK - A walkway upon a wall, protected by a parapet. WARD - A walled defensive enclosure.

INDEX OF CASTLES OF ULSTER